Handbook

A Guide for the Nonspecialist

The Cancer Handbook
A Guide for the Nonspecialist

Darrell E. Ward

In conjunction with

The Ohio State University Comprehensive Cancer Center

Arthur G. James Cancer Hospital and
  Research Institute

and

The Ohio State University
Office of University Communications

Ohio State University Press
Columbus

Disclaimer
The *Cancer Handbook: A Guide for Nonspecialists* is designed for educational purposes only. It is not intended as a substitute for medical advice from a physician. The reader should consult a physician in matters relating to his or her health or that of others.

Earlier version published as *Reporting on Cancer* © 1994 by The Ohio State University.

Library of Congress Cataloging-in-Publication Data

Ward, Darrell E., 1947–
    [Reporting on cancer]
    The cancer handbook : a guide for the nonspecialist / Darrell E. Ward.
        p.   cm.
    First published under title: Reporting on cancer, 1994.
    Includes index.
    ISBN 0-8142-0675-1 (pbk. : alk. paper)
    1. Cancer—Popular works. 2. Cancer—Terminology. 3. Journalism, Medical. I. Title.
    RC263.W33 1995
    616.99'4—dc20
                                                              95-8318
                                                                 CIP

Illustrations by David Schumick

Text design by Beth Yaple McGuffey

Printed by Cushing-Malloy, Ann Arbor, MI

The paper in this book meets the guidelines for permanence and durability of the Committee on Production Guidelines for Book Longevity of the Council on Library Resources. ∞

9 8 7 6 5 4 3 2 1

To cancer patients and their families

Contents

Foreword

In recent years, knowledge and understanding of cancer—it's etiology, prevention, diagnosis, and treatment—have advanced inexorably. In particular, the last decade has seen gigantic strides in the areas of cellular biology and genetics at the molecular level. A welter of complex and confusing science has confronted interested nonspecialists, along with an unfamiliar vocabulary.

This handbook by Darrell E. Ward is a greatly expanded version of a guide produced for The Ohio State University Comprehensive Cancer Center–Arthur G. James Cancer Hospital and Research Institute and intended primarily for journalists. The first part of the volume consists of explanations of cancer-associated concepts, ranging from the role of diet in the disease, through the clinical trials process, the nature of metastasis, the interplay of naturally occurring hormones with tumors, ethnicity and cancer, and some thirty other subjects. The sections are current, detailed, and scrupulously researched. The second part of the book comprises a comprehensive glossary of terms pertaining to cancer. Throughout, Mr. Ward has presented the information in language that is readily understandable by the educated layperson.

The Ohio State University (OSU) is well established as a center for cancer research and cancer-patient care. The OSU Cancer Research Center was founded in 1973, and in 1976 the National Cancer Institute designated it a Comprehensive Cancer Center, at that time one of only eighteen in the United States. NCI-designated Comprehensive Cancer Centers provide access to shared resources to enable productive interdisciplinary research. The ultimate goal of a university Comprehensive Cancer Center is to provide the best in patient care through basic and clinical research and their applications, and to provide cancer education to students and the general public. The OSU Comprehensive Cancer Center currently boasts more than two hundred members from eleven colleges. It is still the only NCI-designated Comprehensive Cancer Center in the state of Ohio. The Arthur G. James Cancer Hospital and Research Institute is the primary patient-care facility for the Comprehensive Cancer Center, and is one of only a handful of freestanding cancer hospitals in the United States. The James admitted its first patients in July 1990. It has since admitted patients from all of Ohio's counties, 44 states, and several nations.

Darrell Ward joined the OSU Office of University Communications as senior medical writer in 1990. As such, he has been frequently and closely involved with the basic scientists and clinicians of the Comprehensive Cancer Center and The James, and from them he has collected his material. His ability to translate technically difficult subject matter into lay language is unparalleled, and his work has contributed to the educational goals of the center. The handbook will prove useful not only to journalists and medical writers and editors but also to health-care professionals such as psychologists, family counselors, social workers, and others involved with caring for patients with cancer. It will also benefit cancer advocates, people in the health-insurance industry, and hospital administrators. Indeed, this book is an invaluable tool for anybody who is not a cancer specialist but who wishes to achieve a deeper understanding of the many facets of the disease.

David E. Schuller, M.D.
Director
Comprehensive Cancer Center
The Arthur G. James Cancer Hospital and Research Institute
The Ohio State University

A Note from the Author

The *Cancer Handbook* is intended to help those with little knowledge of cell or molecular biology understand the science of cancer. It is an expanded version of an earlier edition, *Reporting on Cancer: A Guide for Journalists*, distributed to the media by The Ohio State University Comprehensive Cancer Center. The *Cancer Handbook* contains four additional sections, as well as a some corrections and updating of portions of the text.

The handbook is divided into two parts. The first provides explanations of concepts relating to cancer research, diagnosis, treatment, and prevention. The second part is a glossary of terms. The glossary is followed by a brief list of additional reading that will provide in-depth information on cancer and insights into how basic and clinical research are done.

In using the handbook, one can pick and choose topics of interest, or read it in an organized way for an overview of cancer biology and cancer care. For this purpose, I recommend reading certain sections in the following order: The Cell; DNA; Genes, Mutations, and Chromosomes; Gene Control/Gene Regulation; Proteins and Protein Synthesis; Causes of Cancer; Carcinogenesis; Oncogenes; Tumor Suppressor Genes; Metastasis; Diagnosis of Cancer; Treatment of Cancer; Drug Resistance and Cancer; and "Curing" Cancer. Follow these sections with those on pain control, hospice, risk, and ethnicity and cancer.

Acknowledgments

This handbook brings together information gathered from research papers, textbooks, and interviews with numerous researchers at Ohio State's Comprehensive Cancer Center–Arthur G. James Cancer Hospital and Research Institute. Much of what it contains was learned while writing about cancer research here at Ohio State University and while writing feature stories for *Frontiers*, the magazine published by the OSU cancer program.

My thanks to the clinical and basic researchers with the OSU Comprehensive Cancer Center–Arthur G. James Cancer Hospital and Research Institute for their forbearance as I questioned them during the past five years about the intricacies and implications of their work. In particular, I want to thank the following OSU Comprehenisve Cancer Center researchers and physicians for reviewing portions of the manuscript: Larry Copeland, M.D., professor of obstetrics and gynecology; Reinhard Gahbauer, M.D., professor of radiology; Julian Kim, M.D., associate professor of surgery; Eric Kraut, M.D., professor of internal medicine; George Marzluf, Ph.D., professor and chair of biochemistry; Ronald Siegle, M.D., associate professor of otolaryngology; Gary Stoner, Ph.D., director of basic research programs; Pierre Triozzi, associate professor of internal medicine; Harrison Weed, M.D., assistant professor of internal medicine; Jay Wilkins, Ph.D., associate professor of preventive medicine; and Donn Young, biostatistician. Thanks, too, to copyeditor Ann Elliot, whose review helped strengthen the text. I also want to express gratitude to Beth Yaple McGuffey, senior graphic designer, for designing the book and for being so darn pleasant to work with.

I especially want to thank David Schuller, M.D., director of the OSU Comprehensive Cancer Center and the James Cancer Hospital, for his support and enthusiasm for this project. I owe an equal measure of thanks to Earle Holland, associate executive director of University Communications, for his support during the writing of the handbook.

I welcome suggestions that will make future editions of the *Cancer Handbook* more useful.

Darrell E. Ward
University Communications
1125 Kinnear Road
Columbus, OH 43212-1153
(614) 292-8456

E-mail address: Ward.25@osu.edu

Introduction—What Is Cancer?

Cancer can develop in any tissue of any organ at any time.
The Merck Manual, 15th Edition

Cancer is the name given to more than 100 different types of malignant tumors. It is characterized by uncontrolled cell growth and by the ability of tumor cells to metastasize—to invade neighboring tissues and spread to other areas of the body. This ability separates malignant tumors from benign tumors. Metastatic cells are carried by the blood or lymphatic systems to other areas of the body where they develop into secondary tumors. Metastasis makes cancer difficult to treat. About half of the 1.1 million people diagnosed with cancer in the United States each year die of the disease.

At the same time, about half the people who get cancer survive. A diagnosis of cancer is not an automatic death warrant. Advances in treatment have extended the lives of many patients with chronic disease, advances in pain control have reduced the suffering that cancer patients often endured, and drugs have been developed to ease the side effects of many chemotherapy treatments.

A cancerous tumor is often defined as a "malignant neoplasm." Neoplasm means new growth, which refers to the tumor. Malignant refers to the tumor's ability to spread. Cancerous tumors are classified into three groups, depending on the type of cell in which they originate. **Carcinomas** arise from epithelial tissue; **sarcomas** arise in muscle, connective tissue, and bone; and **lymphomas, leukemias,** and **myelomas** arise in the vascular tissues of the body. Lymphomas are tumors of the lymphatic system; leukemias are tumors of the blood system; and myelomas form in the tissues that give rise to blood cells.

Cancer cells differ from normal cells in their behavior, biochemistry, genetics, and microscopic appearance.

Oncology is the study of cancer.

Animal Models and Cancer Research

The use of animals as models for human disease has been indispensable in understanding the causes, biology, and prevention of cancer. Animal models also play a crucial role in the preclinical testing of new anti-cancer drugs and treatments.

Rodents—mice, rats, and hamsters—are the most commonly used animals for modeling human tumors. (The term "murine," frequently used in scientific papers, refers to rodents, particularly rats and mice.) Rodents have several advantages in medical research: their physiology and genetics are well understood, they are relatively easy and cheap to maintain, and they, like humans, are mammals. In addition:

- Rodents develop cancer relatively easily in response to chemical carcinogens. The tumors also develop rather quickly, over months rather than years, as is the case in larger animals.
- Some strains of rodents develop tumors spontaneously in certain organs. Such tumors often differ biologically from tumors that are induced.
- Tumor cells transplanted from one rodent to another readily go on to form complete tumors.
- Cells removed from rodent tumors have been kept alive for long periods in laboratories around the world. These tumor cell lines are well understood and easily transplanted into animals.
- Human tumor cells often go on to form tumors when transplanted into immunodeficient rodents.

But animal models have their shortcomings, and results obtained through animal experiments must be applied cautiously to humans. Disadvantages to using animals to study human cancers include the following:

- Extensive inbreeding has made many rodent strains genetically similar; humans, on the other hand, are genetically diverse. Thus, mice might respond very similarly in an experiment from one individual to another, whereas humans might respond very differently to the same circumstances from one individual to another.
- Animals and humans have important metabolic, physiological, and hormonal differences. Animals can differ greatly from humans in

what carcinogens they metabolize, how they metabolize them—i.e., what enzymes are used—and in how their cells repair DNA damaged by chemicals. In fact, such differences exist between different species of rodents: some substances can cause cancer in rats, but not in mice or hamsters. One example is the controversy that arose when saccharin was linked to bladder cancer in 1977. Critics claimed that the mechanism that helps saccharin induce cancers in rats didn't apply to humans. Research in 1992 showed they might have been right. Rats, it seems, have from 100 to 1,000 times the concentration of globulin and albumin in their bladders that humans do. And it's the interaction of these two proteins with urine that leads to saccharin-induced bladder cancer.

- Anatomical differences can make it hard to compare animals and humans. For example, differences in the anatomy of the nose make it difficult to use rats to study the effect of formaldehyde exposure on the nasal cavity of humans.

- Practical limitations on the design of animal tests and experiments can make their results difficult to apply to humans. Researchers often expose animals to chemical carcinogens at levels far higher than those encountered by humans, for example. This is often done to reduce the amount of time and expense of an experiment. It may also be done to induce the cancer in enough test animals to show that the effect is statistically real and not due to chance. But it may also exaggerate the hazards of the chemical at low doses (see also "Identifying Carcinogens," page 49).

In 1984, the first strain of transgenic mice was developed. A transgenic mouse—a mouse that contains a gene from another animal—is produced by introducing a foreign gene into the egg that produces the mouse. The transplanted gene then becomes a permanent part of the animal's genetic makeup. In this way, scientists can study the influence of a particular gene on tumor development. Transgenic mice have been produced that develop particular tumors, or that are particularly sensitive to cancer-causing viruses and chemicals. Transgenic mice should prove valuable for testing suspected carcinogens, new cancer treatments, and new measures to prevent cancer.

Transgenic animals also have limitations, however. For example, cancer is thought to arise when a single tumor cell begins proliferating within a bed of normal tissue, overcoming the controls normally imposed by cell-cell contact. In a transgenic animal, the tumor cell is surrounded by non-normal cells, cells that all carry the mutated gene. This difference could make the biology of these tumors different from that of spontaneous tumors.

Cancer Information

Current cancer information is available by telephone, fax machine, and over the internet through one or more of the following sources.

American Cancer Society Cancer Response System : Telephone the ACS Cancer Response System with questions about the signs and symptoms of many cancers, for the location of mammography centers, or to request ACS publications. The service also answers questions about the side effects of certain drugs and treatments. For the toll-free number of the ACS Cancer Response System in your state, look under "American Cancer Society" in the telephone book.

Cancer Information Service: The CIS is a toll free telephone service run by the National Cancer Institute. CIS answers questions about cancer diagnosis, treatment, prevention, and rehabilitation. CIS will also provide NCI literature, and the names of local cancer specialists and of cancer-related services and programs. The offices also have access to NCI's computerized data base, PDQ (Physician Data Query), which contains the latest information on cancer treatment. PDQ also lists about 90 percent of the clinical trials open to cancer patients. To reach the CIS office in your region Monday through Friday, call toll free:
1-800-4-CANCER (1-800-422-6237).

CancerFax: Information from NCI's PDQ database on the treatment of many cancers is available 24 hours a day through CancerFax, an automated fax service. Call CancerFax from the telephone on your fax machine, and a recording will tell you how to proceed. The information is sent immediately. Call CancerFax from the telephone on your fax machine at:
1-301-402-5874.

CancerNet: Information from PDQ is also available by electronic mail through CancerNet. To use CancerNet, first request the contents pages from the following E-mail address:

cancernet@icicb.nci.nih.gov

Leave the "Subject" line of the message blank; the body of the message should consist of one word: help. The contents pages will be sent by return E-mail.

Cansearch: A Guide to Cancer Resources: Cansearch is described as "a guide to cancer resources on the Internet, courtesy of the National Coalition for Cancer Survivorship." It is an excellent starting point for people who are inexperienced in finding information on the internet. It directs users to, and helps them use, a host of information sources including CancerNet, OncoLink (described below), Usenet newsgroups, Listserv mailing lists, and more. Cansearch is available on the World Wide Web (WWW) using the following locator:

http://www.access.digex.net/~mkragen/cansearch.html

Ohio State University Comprehensive Cancer Center–Arthur G. James Cancer Hospital and Research Institute: To learn what treatments are available at the The James Cancer Hospital and for answers to questions about cancer, call the James Cancer Line toll free: *1-800-293-5066*

OncoLink: OncoLink is a electronic library of cancer information established by the University of Pennsylvania Medical Center. It uses World Wide Web and gopher servers to provide cancer information for health-care professionals and patients. OncoLink includes explanations of cancer causes and treatments, clinical-trials news, cancer-related news, even cancer-related poetry, and—on the WWW server—artwork. OncoLink's WWW server also provides instant access to other cancer-related servers.

To access the OncoLink gopher server, work through the gopher menu system (World Wide Gophers, North American Gophers, USA, Pennsylvania) and scroll down to OncoLink. Click on this for OncoLink's main menu.

To access OncoLink's WWW server and home page, use the following locator:

http://cancer.med.upenn.edu/

Carcinogenesis

Carcinogenesis is the origin or initiation of cancer. Most tumors are thought to arise from a single abnormal cell. Cancer results when cancer-causing agents—carcinogens—damage DNA, the molecule that stores genetic information in cells. Damaged DNA can result in a genetic mutation. Some genetic mutations are harmless to cells, some are deadly to cells, and some cause cells to behave abnormally. When carcinogens cause mutations in genes that control cell growth, it can lead to cancer. Genes that lead to cancer when mutated are called oncogenes (see "Oncogenes," page 57). A second category of genes—tumor suppressor genes—also plays an important role in cancer. Normally, these genes suppress cell growth and division unless mutations weaken or destroy their funtion (see "Tumor Suppressor Genes," page 78).

Cancer occurs when carcinogens cause mutations that activate one or more oncogenes and inactivate one or more tumor suppressor genes. How quickly this happens depends in part on the potency of the carcinogen, the length of exposure to it, and the ability of an individual's body to repair the damaged DNA before cancer starts.

Carcinogens can be chemical, physical, or viral. Each type damages DNA differently, and how cancer begins depends on the kind of carcinogen responsible. (In addition, genes in the body can mutate spontaneously. This may make a person more susceptible to damage from carcinogens and increase the odds that that person will develop cancer. See "Heredity and Cancer," page 44.)

Chemical carcinogenesis is thought to occur in two stages: initiation and promotion. Initiation occurs when DNA is damaged beyond repair following exposure to a chemical carcinogen. The damage is thought to occur in a matter of hours or days. Promotion begins when cells containing damaged DNA are exposed to a second class of chemicals known as tumor promoters. Tumor promoters are chemicals that do not themselves damage DNA, but they do cause mutated cells to grow. They may also reduce the ability of cells to repair damaged DNA. Promotion is thought to require several steps and can take a decade or more. It is also thought to be reversible until it reaches a point of no return.

The biochemical changes that cause a cell to become cancerous are still not understood, but pieces of the puzzle are falling into place. Some chemicals initiate cancer directly, but most cancer-causing chemicals are really pre-carcinogens. They become carcinogenic only after they've gotten into the cell and are acted on—are metabolized—by the cell. Metabolism changes the chemicals into different substances, ones that can be more easily flushed from the cell into the bloodstream and eliminated from the body by the kidneys.

But some of those simpler molecules, known as reactive intermediates, end up having an affinity for DNA. They cling to DNA and produce "adducts," or mutations. These adducts can lead to cancer if they occur in certain genes (i.e., oncogenes or tumor suppressor genes). On the other hand, if the cell can eliminate the adduct and repair the damaged DNA, carcinogenesis does not proceed and cancer does not develop.

The process through which the cell converts a pre-carcinogen into a carcinogen is called metabolic activation. (A similar pathway is required to activate many drugs, including acetaminophen.)

Physical carcinogenesis occurs when DNA is damaged by physical carcinogens. These include ultraviolet light; X-rays; gamma rays; electron, proton, or neutron beams; and certain wood and metallic dusts and microscopic synthetic fibers and mineral fibers such as asbestos that are inhaled.

Radiation triggers cancer by damaging DNA either directly or indirectly. Direct damage occurs when radiation breaks chemical bonds in DNA, causing a mutation. Indirect damage occurs when the radiation breaks down other molecules in the cell. This can produce highly reactive compounds—free radicals—that can damage DNA. The mechanism through which cancer is induced by dusts and asbestos fibers is not well understood.

Viral carcinogenesis: Only a few classes of viruses are linked to cancer (see "Viruses and Cancer," page 82). These cause cancer either by introducing an oncogene into the DNA of a cell, or by inserting their own genes into the host cell in a way that disrupts the regulation of cell growth and division.

Causes of Cancer

The major causes of human cancer fall into three categories: chemicals, viruses, and irradiation (see Table 1; and "Carcinogenesis," page 6).

Labeling a substance as cancer causing often generates controversy because of the ramifications it can have on business, industry, and the public. The controversy often occurs because the identification of carcinogens relies on tests using bacteria, laboratory cells, and animals, and many people question how meaningful the results are when applied to humans (see "Identifying Carcinogens," page 49).

While hundreds of chemicals can cause cancer in animals, only 24 are at present known to cause cancer in humans (see Table 2, page 10). Others are known to induce cancerous changes in laboratory cells or cause cancer in animals. Such chemicals may be suspected of causing cancer in humans, they may be linked to or even strongly associated with cancer in humans, but they cannot properly be said to cause cancer in humans. This determination generally requires epidemiologic evidence that comes slowly through case-control studies and cohort studies, especially those that establish a dose-response reaction to the carcinogen.

Table 1. The causes of cancer and the percentage of cancer for which they are responsible worldwide.

Cancer Cause	Human Cancers Worldwide (%)
Chemicals	
In the workplace	2–8
Tobacco	30
Tobacco and asbestos	1
Tobacco and alcohol	5
Diet	30–50
Environmental pollution	2
Viruses	10–15
Irradiation (UV light, medical)	1–5

Chemicals

Chemicals in the workplace: Some occupations carry an unusually high risk of exposure to cancer-causing chemicals. These include the manufacture of dyes and chemicals, the manufacture and repair of leather goods, the manufacture of isopropyl alcohol, and the production of plastics and other petroleum products. Exposure to carcinogens in the workplace is thought to account for 2 to 8 percent of human cancers.

Certain substances found on the job also cause cancer when inhaled as dusts. These include asbestos, zeolite, and nickel. Exposure to hardwood dust during the manufacturing of furniture can lead to cancer of the nasal sinuses.

Tobacco: Tobacco use is thought to be responsible for about a third of all cancer cases. It is associated with cancers of the lung, mouth, throat, esophagus, pancreas, bladder, and kidney. Cured tobacco contains nitrosamines, the leading carcinogens in smokeless tobacco. Tobacco smoke contains a range of proven and suspected carcinogens that include aromatic amines, polonium (which is radioactive), formaldehyde, and cadmium. See "Tobacco and Cancer," page 72.

Tobacco becomes a more potent carcinogen when combined with alcohol consumption or with exposure to asbestos fibers in the workplace.

Tobacco and alcohol/asbestos: Alcohol increases the risk of cancers of the mouth, pharynx, larynx, esophagus, and liver. Risk of cancer is 35 times greater among heavy users of both alcohol and tobacco compared to nonusers. Ethanol (i.e., drinking alcohol) does not cause cancer in laboratory animals, making it difficult to study how it causes cancer in humans. Asbestos exposure increases the risk of lung cancer from tobacco use by about 50 times.

Diet: Substances in the diet are thought to be responsible for a third to a half of all cancers. These chemicals and substances range from aromatic amines and polycyclic hydrocarbons formed by overcooking and charcoal broiling meat. Aflatoxin, a naturally occurring chemical found in some molds that grow on foods, is thought to be a leading cause of liver cancer in developing countries. Chemicals known as free radicals form during the metabolism of certain food components and can damage cells in ways that lead to cancer. High-fat and low-fiber diets are associated with colon and other cancers in developed nations.

But the exact role of diet is hard to pin down. For example, it is difficult to determine exactly what and how much people eat over time. It is also difficult to perform tightly controlled diet studies on large numbers of

Table 2. Substances shown to cause cancer in humans. From the National Toxicology Program's *Seventh Annual Report on Carcinogens: 1994, Summary.*

Aflatoxins
4-Aminobiphenyl
Analgesic mixtures containing phenacetin
Arsenic and certain arsenic compounds
Asbestos
Azathioprine
Benzene
Benzidine
Bis(chloromethyl)ether and technical-grade chloromethyl
    methyl ether
1,4-Butanediol dimethylsulfonate (Myleran)
Chlorambucil
1-(2-chloroethyl)-3-(4-methylcyclohexyl)-1-nitrosourea
    (MeCCNU)
Chromium and certain chromium compounds
Conjugated estrogens
Cyclophosphamide
Diethylstilbestrol
Erionite
Melphalan
Methoxsalen with ultraviolet A therapy (PUVA)
Mustard gas
2-Naphthylamine
Radon
Thorium dioxide
Vinyl chloride

In addition, the report lists 150 more chemical substances and medical treatments that are reasonably thought to be carcinogens.

people and follow those people for longer periods of time. This can be done with animals, but it is difficult to judge how applicable the results are to humans. In addition, the same foods can contain substances suspected of causing or promoting cancer and other substances thought to reduce the risk of cancer. See "Diet and Cancer," page 28.

Environmental pollution: Exposure levels of carcinogens in the general environment are thought to be lower than exposures in the workplace. The data are limited, but environmental pollution is thought to be responsible for about 2 percent of cancer deaths. The major atmospheric pollutants are aromatic hydrocarbons produced by the burning of wood, tobacco, and fossil fuels. Chlorinated compounds are important water pollutants linked to cancer in animals. See "Pollution of the Environment and Cancer," page 64.

Medicines and synthetic hormones: A number of these are known to cause cancer in humans or are strongly linked to the disease. They include certain anti-cancer drugs, particularly the alkylating agents such as cyclophosphamide and chlorambucil; anabolic steroids; immunosuppressants such as azathioprine and cyclosporine; synthetic estrogens such as diethylstilbestrol; conjugated estrogens; and estrogen-containing contraceptives.

Viruses

A small number of viruses are strongly linked to human cancers. They include the hepatitis B virus (HBV), the Epstein-Barr virus (EBV), the human papilloma virus (HPV), the human T-cell lymphotropic virus Type 1 (HTLV-1), the human T-cell lymphotropic virus Type 2 (HTLV-2), and the human immunodeficiency virus (HIV). See "Viruses and Cancer," page 82.

Irradiation

Atomic—or ionizing—radiation and ultraviolet radiation from sunlight can cause cancer. An increased risk of cancer is associated with high doses of ionizing radiation, such as from nuclear explosions and those used for treatment of certain diseases. The risk of cancer appears to be low for low doses of X-rays received during diagnostic procedures.

Radon is a radioactive gas that results from the disintegration of the element radium. Radium occurs naturally in low amounts in bedrock and certain rock formations. Radon gas accumulates in caves, mines, and other spaces that have limited air circulation. It can also accumulate in tightly sealed, energy-efficient houses and houses with basements. At one time, radon was thought to pose a high risk of lung cancer for these homeowners. But the extent of the danger remains unresolved. As of early 1992, radon was thought responsible for as many as 16,000 lung cancer deaths annually in the U.S., mainly among smokers. But this conclusion involves numerous assumptions, and, as one prominent cancer researcher put it, "no convincing epidemiologic study has yet been performed."

Ultraviolet light: see "Ultraviolet Light, Ozone, Tanning Beds, and Cancer," page 80.

The Cell

A human cell is like a walled medieval city that sits beside a river. In the center is a castle, also surrounded by a wall. The castle is the heart of the city, the seat of its government, and the center of its commerce.

It is a thriving city. Orders for goods and services are received at the castle. The orders are processed, and instructions and blueprints for what is needed are sent to manufacturing sites outside the castle wall. Assembly lines are set up to produce the necessary goods. Some of the products remain in the city to maintain its infrastructure; others are sent to the river for export. The river, in fact, gives life to the city. It brings fuel for power and raw materials for manufacturing, and it takes away waste. It is also a channel of communication, carrying condition reports, orders for supplies, and commands to grow or to specialize in some way.

The river, of course, represents a capillary, a microscopic tributary of the circulatory system. The outer wall is the cell membrane, and the castle is the cell nucleus surrounded by the nuclear membrane. The area between the nucleus and the cell membrane is the cell cytoplasm.

The records within the castle are the genes, which are made of DNA. The DNA is in long thread-like strands. Each strand is a chromosome, and each chromosome contains thousands of genes. (Most human cells have 46 chromosomes—two sets of 23—and an estimated 100,000 genes; eggs and sperm each have one set of 23 chromosomes).

The "goods" produced by cells are primarily proteins. Each gene contains instructions for making one protein. When a protein is needed by the cell, the gene for that protein is turned on—activated—and a blueprint of the gene is made in the form of a ticker-tape-like strand of messenger RNA (mRNA). The mRNA travels to the cytoplasm. There it becomes the basis of an assembly line for production of the protein. Tiny two-lobed structures called ribosomes attach to the "start" end of the mRNA and move down its length, reading the encoded structure of the protein. On the basis of this code, amino acids are attached one to another like chemical snap beads. The sequence of amino acids gives the protein its properties (see "Proteins and Protein Synthesis," page 66).

The Cell Membrane

The cell membrane (or plasma membrane) is an organelle of the cell that plays an important role in cancer. It is composed of a double layer of lipid molecules. The lipid molecules that make up the cell membrane are often pictured as having a round head and a twin tail. In the cell membrane, these molecules lie side by side—heads out, tails in—to form a double layer known as a lipid bilayer (Fig. 1). A lipid is a fat-like substance, and lipid bilayers are fluid-like. Puncture one with a needle and it doesn't break. Rather, when the needle is withdrawn, the molecules flow together and fill the hole.

The lipid bilayer provides the structural framework of the cell membrane. From the outside, the cell appears like an enormous ball covered by marbles. Penetrating this marble surface are potato-shaped and spaghetti-like objects. These are protein molecules that carry out the activities of the membrane. Most membrane proteins fall into three groups: transport, recognition, and receptor proteins.

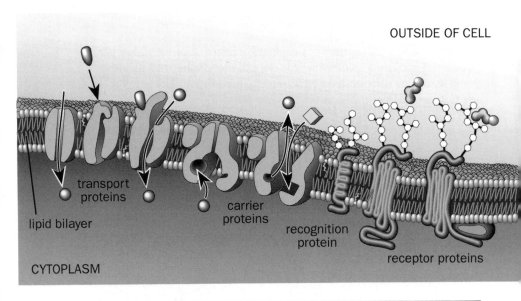

OUTSIDE OF CELL

transport proteins

lipid bilayer

carrier proteins

recognition protein

receptor proteins

CYTOPLASM

Figure 1. The cell membrane consists of two layers of lipid molecules—the lipid bilayer. Protein molecules are embedded in this lipid bilayer. The proteins serve a variety of functions. Transport and carrier proteins control what goes into and out of the cell, sometimes under the influence of a second molecule; recognition proteins help identify the cell to other cells; and receptor proteins trigger changes within the cell. The tiny lipids with crooked tails are molecules of cholesterol.

Transport proteins help regulate what gets into the cell. Some form pores in the membrane that are always open; others work like gates to control the movement of molecules into and out of the cell. Others, known as carrier proteins, attach to certain molecules and bring them into the cell.

Transport proteins are responsible for making some types of cancers resistant to chemotherapeutic drugs. The transport protein called p-glycoprotein, for example, becomes highly active in some cancer cells, pumping the drug out of the cell before it has a chance to kill the cell.

Recognition proteins function like molecular flags and signposts. They allow cells to identify and interact with one other. Recognition proteins often have branched, stick-like projections made of sugar that project from the cell membrane into the surrounding space (protein molecules that include sugar are known as glycoproteins).

Recognition proteins allow sperm to recognize eggs of the same species, allow viruses and bacteria to identify the proper cells to infect, and provide sites where one cell attaches to another. Toxins bind to recognition proteins to kill cells.

Immune-system cells such as T cells use recognition proteins to tell whether a given cell is part of the body or not. Transplanted organs have the wrong recognition proteins, so the body rejects the transplanted tissue unless the immune system is suppressed.

Recognition proteins—and the lack of them—play important roles in cancer. Normally, cell-cell contacts made through recognition proteins help regulate cell growth. Cancer cells overcome these controls to form a tumor and to metastasize. Cancer cells may also produce recognition proteins that normally appear in other types of cells and use those counterfeit proteins to aid metastasis. At the same time, cancer cells have few recognition proteins unique to themselves, so the immune system doesn't recognize them as cells that should be destroyed. A major goal of cancer research is to identify recognition proteins that are unique to cancer cells and to increase their number. This may cause the immune system to regard the tumor as foreign and to destroy it. Knowing the structure of recognition proteins for cancer cells would also make it possible to design drugs specific for these proteins and, therefore, specific for cancer cells.

Receptor proteins are molecular switches that turn on or turn off some activity in the cell when activated by certain molecules that link to them. Cell membranes have receptor proteins for hormones and growth factors that trigger changes in cell growth, for example. Mutations that lead to overproduction of a receptor protein for a growth factor may play a role in some cancers.

Organelles of the Cell

Cells have many specialized parts—organelles—in addition to the nucleus and cell membrane that perform specific functions. Here are some examples:

- Mitochondria combine oxygen with food molecules to produce the energy that powers the cell. They are oval-shaped structures about the size of bacteria.
- The endoplasmic reticulum is a network of sheets, sacks, and channels involved in the production of lipids and proteins.
- The Golgi complex is a system of flattened sacs involved in modifying and packaging materials produced by the cell for secretion or for delivery to other organelles.
- Lysosomes are membrane-bound capsules of enzymes involved in digestion of material within the cell.

Cell Division (Mitosis)

Cells multiply by dividing in two. About a million billion (10^{15}) cell divisions occur to turn a fertilized egg into an adult human being. The process of cell division—mitosis—is normally under tight control by the cell itself. Loss of regulation of cell growth and cell division is a primary cause of cancer.

Before a cell divides, each of its 46 chromosomes—and each of the 100,000 genes—must be exactly duplicated. During cell division, one full set of chromosomes must be correctly distributed to each of the two resulting daughter cells. Organelles in the cell must also be produced and distributed to each of two new cells. Many chemotherapeutic drugs work by blocking cell division, thereby killing the cell.

The Cell Cycle

Cell division is one stage in a four-part cycle that cells go through as they grow and divide. The cell cycle is represented as follows:

G_1: period of cell growth

S: DNA is duplicated

G_2: cell prepares to divide

M: cell division (mitosis)

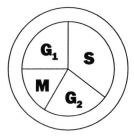

The cell cycle plays an important role in the timing and effectiveness of chemotherapy. Most chemotherapeutic drugs work by blocking cell division. The drug works only on those cells that are in the appropriate phase of the cell cycle for that particular drug. Tumor cells not in the correct phase survive any one administration of the drug. So the timing of subsequent drug treatments and the number of cycles of treatment needed are designed in part around the number of cells undergoing cell division and the pace of the cell cycle for that particular tumor.

Cell Differentiation and Dedifferentiation

The fertilized egg divides to become an embryo and then a fetus. As it does so, cells specialize—differentiate—to form muscles, nerves, bones, and other tissues.

Cell differentiation goes on in some tissues throughout life (for example, in the skin, in the lining of the gut, and in cells that give rise to blood cells). In these tissues, stem cells give rise to intermediate cells that divide a number of times to form cells that then become highly specialized. Stem cells in the circulatory system, for example, divide into two daughter cells. One of these remains a stem cell, but the other divides further to produce cells that mature into lymphocytes, monocytes, neutrophils, or red blood cells. As these cells become specialized—as they differentiate—they lose the ability to divide, and they die within days or weeks.

In many cancers, the control of this normal process is lost. The stem cell may fail to produce intermediate cells, and instead continues to divide to form a tumor. Or, the normal controls on the intermediate cell are lost, and it proliferates wildly to produce a tumor. When these controls are lost in cells that give rise to blood cells, leukemia or lymphoma can result.

The cells that are dividing are thought to be stuck in, or to have returned to, an immature state, and are said to be dedifferentiated. The degree of dedifferentiation can be gauged by the microscopic appearance of the cancer cell. Generally, the less differentiated the tumor cells (i.e., the more dedifferentiated), the more malignant the tumor.

The degree of differentiation is also important in determining the malignancy of solid tumors. Cells in solid tumors can form features found in the normal tissue in which the tumor develops. For example, cells from thyroid tumors may form follicles like the healthy tissue, cells from breast tumors may form duct-like tubules, tumors originating in glands may have mucous cells and tubules, and skin cancer tumors may have cells that make keratin. Tumors that express characteristics of the healthy tissue are said to be well-differentiated tumors. And these tend to be less malignant than undifferentiated tumors.

Chemotherapy for Cancer

Chemotherapy is the use of drugs to kill cancer cells. Most chemotherapeutic drugs are cytotoxic—they work by killing cells. They do this by preventing the formation of new DNA or by blocking some other essential function in the cell. Recent research indicates that some drugs work by causing cells to commit biochemical suicide, a process known as apoptosis. Unfortunately, cytotoxic drugs also kill healthy dividing cells—such as those lining the intestines, in hair follicles, and among blood cells in the bone marrow. This causes the nausea, vomiting, hair loss, and drop in numbers of white blood cells that often accompanies chemotherapy.

Chemotherapy is most effective against tumors with rapidly dividing cells such as leukemia, lymphoma, and Hodgkin's disease. By comparison, the cells of solid tumors divide relatively slowly, and chemotherapy is often less effective against them. In addition, chemotherapy kills only a certain fraction of cells growing in a tumor at any one time—cells that are at a certain stage in the cell cycle (see "The Cell," page 13). No matter how high the dose of drug, if the cancer cell is not in the correct stage of its growth cycle, the drug won't affect it. This is why many tumors are not treated by chemotherapy alone. The primary treatment for breast cancer, for example, is surgery that is then followed by chemotherapy. The chemotherapy—known as adjuvant chemotherapy—is intended to kill any tiny tumors that may have arisen elsewhere in the body (i.e., distant metastases). The rate of cell division is relatively high in these "occult" tumors, making them more susceptible to cytotoxic drugs.

Most chemotherapeutic drugs fall into four classes: alkylating agents, anti-metabolites, plant alkaloids, and antitumor antibiotics.

Alkylating agents are compounds chemically similar to mustard gas. They work by preventing DNA from uncoiling, thereby blocking DNA replication and cell division. This leads to cell death. Alkylating agents include nitrogen mustard and cyclophosphamide. They are important in the treatment of Hodgkin's disease, non-Hodgkin's lymphoma, multiple myeloma, leukemias, breast cancer, prostate cancer, and some lung cancers.

Anti-metabolites masquerade as building blocks of DNA and other vital components of the cell. Some, for example, prevent DNA from replicating properly, thereby killing the cell. Examples include 5-fluorouracil and methotrexate.

Plant alkaloids inhibit cell division by preventing formation of the microtubules critical to mitosis. Examples include vincristine, vinblastine, and colchicine.

Antitumor antibiotics block cell division by binding to DNA and preventing the double helix from unwinding for replication. Some inhibit the enzymes needed for DNA synthesis. Examples include doxorubicin, bleomycin, mitomycin, and cisplatin.

Chemotherapy with Unusual Mechanisms of Action

- L-asparaginase, an enzyme, is used to treat acute lymphoblastic leukemias (ALL). ALL cells, unlike normal cells, require an outside source of the amino acid asparagine to grow. The enzyme depletes the supply of asparagine in the cell and prevents ALL cells from growing.
- Taxol is a drug derived from the bark of the Pacific yew tree that prevents microtubules from disassembling during cell division, killing cancer cells. Taxol was approved by the FDA in December 1992 for treatment of ovarian cancer.
- Tamoxifen is used to treat recurrent and early-stage breast cancer. It is also being tested to determine if it will prevent breast cancer in women at high risk for the disease. Tamoxifen has a chemical structure similar to the hormone estrogen, which is needed by many breast tumors to grow (see "Hormones and Cancer," page 46). Tamoxifen does not kill tumor cells, and for this reason it lacks many of the severe side effects of cytotoxic anti-cancer drugs. Rather, it seems to work by occupying estrogen receptors found on cells in ER+ breast tumors. In effect, it puts the cells in a chemically induced state of suspended animation.

Promising Experimental Approaches

The following are examples of the strategies now being pursued by researchers; the list is not intended to be inclusive.

- Aromatase inhibitors block the production of the hormone estrogen. Aromatase is a natural enzyme required by the body to produce estrogen. Aromatase inhibitors block that enzyme, thereby halting the production of estrogen and slowing the growth of estrogen-dependent breast cancers.

- Camptothecins are enzyme inhibitors that work by blocking an enzyme needed by DNA to uncoil for cell division. The drug topotecan is one example. Topotecan blocks one of the actions of the enzyme topoisomerase 1, which causes nicks along DNA. The nicks relieve stresses that build up as the DNA molecule unwinds in preparation for cell division. Afterward, the enzyme would normally also repair the nicks. But topotecan attaches to the enzyme and blocks the repair action, thereby killing the cell. Clinical trials for this drug are under way.
- Trans-retinoic acid is an experimental drug derived from vitamin A. Like a stuck phonograph that plays the same thing over and over, cancer cells are stuck in a stage of cell growth and division. Trans-retinoic acid works not by killing cancer cells outright but by pushing them on to maturity and death. The drug shows promise for treatment of squamous cell carcinoma and acute promyelocytic leukemia. Clinical trials are under way.
- Gene therapy is being used to make tumor cells specifically sensitive to chemotherapeutic drugs. One example involves transplanting a gene for herpes into tumor cells. This makes the cancer cells sensitive to the anti-herpes drug ganciclovir, which is given by intravenous injection. Clinical trials began in March 1993 in 15 patients with terminal brain tumors.
- Immunotoxins are bacterial or plant toxins coupled to antibodies specific for cancer cells. The toxins kill by arresting protein synthesis. Researchers hope that this method of cell killing will prevent cancer cells from becoming resistant to the drugs, which is a problem with conventional chemotherapy.
- Enediynes (pronounced EEN-dye-ines) are naturally occurring, cancer-fighting drugs that are being redesigned in the laboratory to make them highly specific for cancer cells. They work by pulling hydrogen atoms from the DNA molecule, causing it to collapse. A designed enediyne molecule has three subunits: an enediyne core, which is the reactive part of the molecule; a delivery system, which recognizes and attaches to a cancer cell; and a triggering device, which initiates the chemical reaction that destroys the DNA molecule. Enediynes have been tested on leukemia and other cancer cell lines cultured in the laboratory—but they are years away from being used in human volunteers. The drugs showed relatively high activity against the cancer cells and relatively low activity toward various normal cell lines. These drugs are highly experimental.
- Antisense therapy is an experimental means of blocking the action of specific genes. It uses laboratory-produced single-strand lengths of DNA to block messenger RNA (mRNA). The DNA strands are short—only 15 to 30 base pairs long—and are complementary to the mRNA being targeted. The short pieces of DNA bind to the mRNA, thereby blocking production of protein.

Clinical Trials and Drug Development

Clinical trials are an integral part of the drug development and approval process. The randomized clinical trial is the gold standard for judging the safety and effectiveness of new drugs and treatments.

Clinical trials are performed by the National Cancer Institute (NCI) and at comprehensive cancer centers and other health centers, usually through clinical trials cooperative groups (see "Clinical Trials Cooperative Groups," page 24). A clinical trial can be conducted at a single hospital, or at dozens of health centers in several nations. Every physician participating in the trial receives a rule book—a research protocol—that carefully outlines which patients are to be accepted and how their treatment is to be administered.

The Food and Drug Administration (FDA) requires that all new drugs demonstrate their safety and effectiveness through the clinical trials process before they can be approved for marketing. In these cases, drug companies also conduct trials (or contract the work to medical schools). The FDA studies the results of clinical trials; it does not conduct them.

Promising new substances first undergo pre-clinical testing in animals for toxicity and pharmacological activity. If a substance shows good results in these tests, the FDA will designate it an Investigational New Drug (IND). It can then go into clinical testing on human volunteers. (The adjective "clinical" indicates tests that use people as opposed to animal or other laboratory tests.) Clinical trials are conducted in three phases:

- **Phase 1 trials** mark the first time the substance is taken by humans. The objective is to establish that it is safe and can be tolerated by the human body. The initial dosages are based on the earlier animal studies. The test lasts several months to a year and uses 20 to 100 healthy volunteers.

- **Phase 2 trials** provide early evidence that the new drug is effective in humans in specific types of cancer. A Phase 2 trial lasts several months to two years and can use several hundred volunteers. Occasionally, a new drug shows dramatic effectiveness during the Phase 2 trial and earns FDA approval without further testing.

- **Phase 3 trials** are designed to demonstrate whether the new drug is more effective than the treatment already available. Again, the drug's safety is also being tested, but in a much larger and more varied group of patient volunteers, often thousands, at health centers around the U.S. and Canada. A Phase 3 trial is also a *randomized* clinical trial; that is, patients are assigned randomly—often by a computerized flip of the coin—to either a group receiving the experimental treatment or to a control group, which receives the standard treatment. Comparing the two groups in terms of survival, tumor shrinkage, or some other indicator at the end of the trial determines whether the new drug is better than the standard treatment.

Results of a randomized trial determine whether general use of the drug is justified. If so, the manufacturer submits a New Drug Application to the FDA. The FDA will then likely approve the drug for treatment of the disease for which it was tested during the clinical trial. (The drug is not limited to that use, however. Once a drug is approved, individual physicians can use it to treat other diseases for which they feel the drug might be beneficial. This is known as "off-label drug use.")

Clinical Trials Cooperative Groups

Clinical Trials Cooperative Groups (also referred to as Clinical Cooperative Groups or Cancer Study Groups) were organized by the National Cancer Institute to generate and conduct clinical trials of new cancer treatments. The groups are composed of Comprehensive Cancer Centers, medical school hospitals, and large public hospitals. More than 2,200 institutions and 16,000 individual investigators participate in the program.

The cooperative group program began in 1955; in 1986, the program was formally designated the Clinical Trials Cooperative Group Program under the NCI's Division of Cancer Treatment. In fiscal year 1989, the NCI awarded over $57.4 million to cooperative group research.

Some clinical cooperative groups focus on treatment of a single type of cancer; some study a specific type of cancer therapy; others concentrate on a group of related cancers. The following is a list of Clinical Trials Cooperative Groups as of March 1993:

Brain Tumor Cooperative Group
Cancer and Leukemia Group B (CALGB)
Children's Cancer Study Group (CCSG)
Eastern Cooperative Oncology Group (ECOG)
European Organization for Research on Treatment for Cancer (EORTC)
Gynecologic Oncology Group (GOG)
Intergroup Rhabdomyosarcoma Study Group
National Surgical Adjuvant Breast and Bowel Project (NSABP)
National Wilms' Tumor Study Group
North Central Cancer Treatment Group
Pediatric Oncology Group (POG)
Radiation Therapy Oncology Group (RTOG)
Southwest Oncology Group (SWOG)

Another NCI program, the Community Clinical Oncology Program (CCOP), makes experimental therapies available to people who are receiving treatment in their communities and are unable to travel to a major medical center. Begun in 1983, the CCOP allows community physicians to participate in NCI-approved clinical trials. The physicians must be affiliated with a clinical cooperative group or an NCI-designated cancer center.

"Curing" Cancer

Generally speaking, most oncologists are reluctant to use the word "cured" in reference to cancer. They speak instead of survival rates—probabilities based on survival studies. Cancer survival rates are usually given as the percentage of people surviving after five years following treatment. The odds that a particular kind of cancer will not recur depend on the kind of cancer and the extent of the disease when treated. Extent of disease refers to whether the patient was treated for local disease (confined to the organ in which it originated), regional disease (spread to nearby lymph nodes), or distant disease (secondary tumors occurring in other areas of the body).

The 1992 five-year relative survival rates for malignant melanoma, for example, were 91 percent for local, 50 percent for regional, and 14 percent for distant disease. This would be interpreted to mean that 91 percent of people diagnosed and treated for melanoma that was still confined to the skin were alive after five years. Of people diagnosed and treated for distant disease, however, only 14 percent remained alive after five years.

Cancer survival rates are probabilities based on survival studies. Actually, two types of survival rates—observed and relative—can be given. Observed, or absolute, survival is the actual proportion of people alive after five years (or whatever time period is used). Those who are not alive, however, could have died from cancer or from other causes—from heart attacks or car accidents, for example. Relative survival compensates for such losses. As a result, relative survival rates are higher than observed survival rates. The observed five-year survival rate in the United States for all cancer in 1991 was 40 percent, but when this number is adjusted to account for those who died of other causes, the average relative survival rate becomes 50 percent.

Diagnosis of Cancer

Cancer diagnosis begins when a person notices something that suggests cancer is present—a lump under the skin, blood in the stool, a change in a mole—and goes to a doctor. Cancer may also be found when a physician notices something suspicious during a physical exam, a screening exam, or treatment for some unrelated medical problem. An individual suspected of having cancer should see an oncologist, who will coordinate the tests needed for diagnosis (i.e., a diagnostic program) and develop a treatment plan (see "Treatment of Cancer," page 73).

An exam by an oncologist begins with a detailed patient history. Laboratory tests usually include blood counts and blood chemistry. The analysis of blood chemistry includes measurement of serum tumor markers, chemicals present at higher than normal levels when certain cancers are present (see "Tumor Markers, Serum," page 75). A patient may be referred to a radiologist for imaging tests—X-rays, mammograms, scintigrams, ultrasound, and computed tomography (CT) and magnetic resonance imaging (MRI) scans. These help locate and stage the malignancy. But imaging tests also have their shortcomings. CT and MRI scans, for example, accurately determine the presence or extent of many tumor types only about 60 percent of the time.

Malignancies located in hollow organs—the esophagus, larynx, bronchi, stomach, large intestine, urinary bladder, and vagina—can often be inspected, photographed, and biopsied (see below) by medical specialists using the appropriate instruments. The results of such tests are given to the oncologist, who uses them to aid in diagnosis and to determine treatment.

A definite diagnosis of cancer cannot occur—and treatment should not begin—until tissue has been removed from the tumor and microscopically examined by a pathologist who confirms that malignant cells are present. The pathologist may also grade the cells for aggressiveness (see "Tumor Staging and Grading," page 76). The removal of living cells, tissues, or fluids for the purpose of making a diagnosis is a biopsy. Biopsies can be done in several ways depending on the size and type of tumor:

Fine-needle aspiration uses a fine needle and syringe to suction clumps of cells from a tumor. It requires a large tumor that is not near a major blood vessel or hollow organ, and can often be done without anesthesia.

Needle biopsy uses a large-bore needle and local anesthetic to obtain a small core of tissue.

Incisional biopsy is surgical removal of a small area of tissue. It can often be performed with local anesthesia on an outpatient basis.

Excisional biopsy is the surgical removal of an entire tumor for analysis. It requires local or general anesthetic and is frequently used for breast tumors less than about an inch in diameter. Also called a lumpectomy.

Cancer cells from breast and prostate tumors will be further tested for the presence or absence of estrogen or androgen receptors. The absence of receptors generally indicates a more aggressive form of the disease.

Sometimes, the true extent of a tumor's development isn't known until a patient undergoes surgery. At that point, the surgical oncologist can determine the size of a tumor and the extent of its spread, a process known as tumor staging. It helps determine a patient's prognosis, what therapy is appropriate, and whether the therapy is working (see "Tumor Staging and Grading," page 76).

Many of the diagnostic steps described above are also used to evaluate the recurrence of cancer following treatment.

Diet and Cancer

Some foods and food components have been associated with an increase in the risk of cancer, while others appear to decrease the risk. Evidence comes from laboratory and epidemiological research. Laboratory research has used animals (primarily rats and mice) and cells cultured in the laboratory. Epidemiological evidence comes from comparison of cancer incidence rates between nations and between regions within nations. An estimated 35 percent of cancer deaths are thought to be associated with foods.

Dietary components that influence cancer risk can be foods consumed in relatively large quantities (macronutrients), such as fat and fiber, or they may be organic substances required in the diet in small quantities (micronutrients), such as vitamins.

Factors associated with an increased risk of cancer

include high levels of fat, salt, calories, and alcohol, and low levels of fiber and important nutrients. Cancer risk is also increased by the presence of carcinogens in food from natural sources and environmental contamination, and carcinogens introduced during cooking or processing.

Dietary fat increases the risk of colon and rectal cancer. It is thought that a 50 percent reduction of animal fat would cut the rate of colon cancer in half. An association between a high fat diet and cancer of the breast, endometrium, ovary, and prostate (hormone-related cancers) is less clear. The evidence is mainly epidemiological. Western nations, where the diet can be 35–45 percent fat, have high rates of breast and prostate cancer. In Japan and other southeast Asian nations, where the diet is only about 15 percent fat, the incidence of these cancers is low. Dietary fat is thought to be a cancer promoter (see "Carcinogenesis," page 6).

Alcohol consumption—heavy use of beer, wine, and spirits, particularly by people who smoke—increases the risk of cancers of the mouth, throat, larynx, liver, and esophagus (and possibly of the breast and colorectum).

Salt and pickling are associated with high rates of cancer of the esophagus, stomach, and nasopharynx. Stomach and nasopharyngeal cancers are rare in the U.S. but high in countries such as China where salted fish and pickled vegetables are eaten in relatively large quantities.

Naturally occurring carcinogens include aflatoxins produced by molds that grow on stored nuts, grains, and other foodstuffs. Edible mushrooms contain hydrazines, and some herbal teas contain tannins. Some flavorings and spices contain alkyl benzenes.

Carcinogens from environmental contamination include chemicals that are taken up by animals and plants. They include pesticides such as DDT and chlordane; components of petroleum such as polyaromatic hydrocarbons; and industrial pollutants such as arsenic, asbestos, heavy metals, and PCBs (polychlorinated biphenyls). Many of the chemicals are soluble in fat, so that when eaten by an animal they accumulate in fatty tissue rather than being flushed from the body.

Carcinogens introduced during cooking and processing include aromatic amines and polycyclic hydrocarbons produced when meat is charbroiled. In the stomach, nitrites added as food preservatives can interact with naturally occurring amines in foods to form nitrosamines, which are thought to cause cancer.

Factors associated with a decreased risk of cancer

include fiber and a number of micronutrients and natural chemicals. Substances in cabbage, broccoli, cauliflower, mustard greens, and kale reduce the activity of the hormone estrogen, a tumor promoter. Terpenes in citrus fruits slow cholesterol production and stimulate enzymes that block carcinogens. Polyacetylenes in parsley slow production of prostaglandin, also a tumor promoter. Sulfur compounds in garlic retard tumor development; and peanuts, beans, and peas have compounds that turn off cancer-gene enzymes and block estrogen receptors.

Fiber is plant material that cannot be broken down by the digestive system. It includes cellulose in plant cell walls, pectin and other complex plant sugars, and methyl cellulose. Fiber is thought to fight cancer by adding bulk to the feces. It dilutes or absorbs carcinogens in the feces, reduces the degree of contact between carcinogens and the wall of the colon, and speeds the movement of feces through the colon.

Micronutrients in fresh fruits and vegetables are thought to reduce the risk of cancer in a number of ways. Examples include the following:

- Antioxidants are thought to protect cells against damage caused by highly reactive chemicals known as oxygen radicals. Antioxidants include vitamins C and E, and carotenoids such as beta-carotene.
- Indoles, isothiocyanates, and limonoids boost the activity of protective enzymes. Indoles and isothiocyanates are found in cabbage, broccoli, and related vegetables; limonoids are found in citrus fruits.

- Isothiocyanates and other agents reduce the activity of enzymes in the cell that leads to the formation of substances that damage DNA.
- Vitamin A derivatives push cancer cells to a greater state of maturity (i.e., to differentiate), slowing their rate of cell division.

Other micronutrients slow the production of some hormones or block the action of hormones on cancer cells.

DNA

DNA (deoxyribonucleic acid) is the molecule that stores genetic information in cells. Each chromosome in a cell is one long, tightly coiled molecule of DNA that has a variety of proteins associated with it.

A molecule of DNA resembles a ladder twisted to form a helix (Fig. 2). The two outer strands of the ladder are made of alternating sugar and phosphate molecules. The rungs of the ladder are composed of pairs of chemical units called bases. Four bases are found in DNA: adenine (A), cytosine (C), guanine (G), and thymine (T). Through the arrangement of bases in DNA, a gene carries the information needed by the cell to produce a protein (see "Proteins and Protein Synthesis," page 66).

The bases form the ladder rungs in complementary pairs—adenine always pairs across from thymine, and cytosine always pairs across from guanine. Complementary base pairing is an important feature of both DNA and RNA, or ribonucleic acid (as a point of interest, the base thymine is not found in RNA; in its place is the base uracil).

Complementary base pairing allows for the high degree of accuracy required when DNA replicates (i.e., when chromosomes duplicate) prior to cell division. It also allows for the high degree of accuracy needed when genes are copied for the production of proteins by the cell (see "Proteins and Protein Synthesis," page 66). Genetic mutations involve the loss or exchange of bases during DNA replication (see "Genes, Mutations, and Chromosomes," page 40).

Scientists take advantage of complementary base pairing to identify genes and mutations using recombinant DNA technology.

- A researcher who knows the sequence of bases running down one side of the DNA ladder can readily determine the sequence of bases that make up the opposite side.
- A researcher who knows the sequence of bases of a messenger RNA (mRNA) isolated from the cell can work backward from it to determine the sequence of bases in the gene coding for that mRNA.
- A researcher who knows the sequence of bases in a gene can determine its location in a chromosome (i.e., in a strand of DNA). This is done using complementary DNA, or cDNA, a single strand of

DNA made in the laboratory and labeled with radioactive atoms. When cDNA is added to disrupted molecules of DNA from a cell, the cDNA will bind to the cellular DNA where complementary base pairing exists, thereby identifying the location of the gene. Researchers can use this technique to reveal the presence of a mutation in biopsied tumor tissue.

- A researcher who knows the sequence of amino acids in a protein can work backward and determine the sequence of bases in the gene responsible for that protein—and then use cDNA to locate the gene.

Figure 2 (opposite). The DNA double helix (left side of diagram) and DNA replication. Before a cell divides, each strand of DNA—each chromosome—must be duplicated. This process is known as DNA replication. It begins when the strands of the DNA molecule unwind and separate down the center, exposing the two lines of bases like the teeth on each side of an open zipper. This work is done by the enzyme DNA helicase (1). Each open edge serves as a template for formation of a new strand. The new partner strands form along each open edge through complementary base pairing, with adenine units pairing with thymine (and vice versa), and cytosine pairing with guanine. The addition of the bases begins with the help of the enzyme DNA primase (2). Assembly of the new chains is done by the enzyme DNA polymerase (3). The enzyme DNA ligase links short DNA segments together (4).

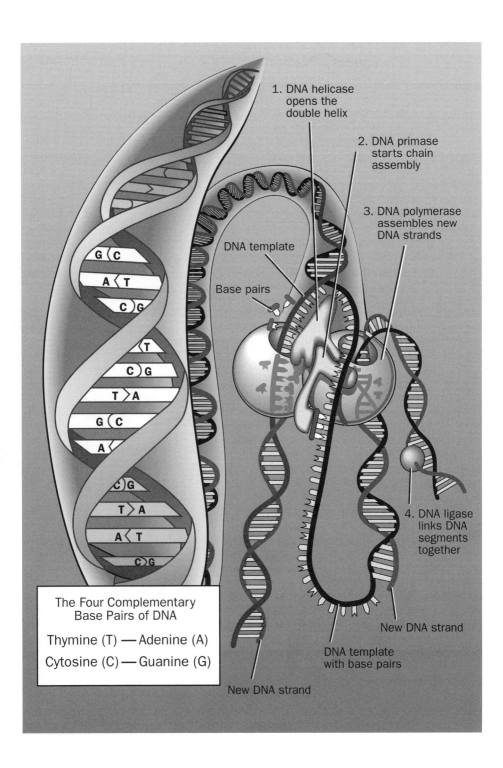

1. DNA helicase opens the double helix

2. DNA primase starts chain assembly

3. DNA polymerase assembles new DNA strands

DNA template

Base pairs

4. DNA ligase links DNA segments together

New DNA strand

DNA template with base pairs

New DNA strand

The Four Complementary Base Pairs of DNA

Thymine (T) — Adenine (A)

Cytosine (C) — Guanine (G)

Drug Resistance and Cancer

Cancer cells frequently develop an almost uncanny ability to resist the effects of anticancer drugs. If cancer chemotherapy fails, it is usually because cancer cells in the tumor have mutated and become resistant to the drug or drugs being given. During treatment, tumor cells susceptible to the chemotherapy are killed. Meanwhile, a few cells in the tumor mutate and became drug resistant. The resistant cells multiply, and the tumor becomes unresponsive to the treatment. Ironically, some of the mechanisms cancer cells harness to resist chemotherapeutic drugs probably evolved in cells to fight natural carcinogens in the environment.

One mechanism leading to drug resistance in cancer cells is gene amplification. In gene amplification, a cancer cell produces perhaps several hundred copies of a particular gene. That, in turn, triggers overproduction of a protein that renders the anticancer drug ineffective.

Other biochemical mechanisms that lead to drug resistance include the following:

- The cancer cell may pump the drug out of the cell as fast as it comes in. This action is carried out by a molecule called p-glycoprotein.
- The cell may stop taking up the drug because the protein molecule that once transported the drug across the cell membrane stops working.
- Many drugs work by causing breaks in the DNA molecule; the cancer cell may respond by developing a highly efficient mechanism for repairing breaks in DNA.
- Certain drugs must be activated by the cell in order to work; some cancer cells develop ways to block or prevent that activation.
- Alternatively, cancer cells may develop a mechanism that inactivates the drug.

Ethnicity and Cancer

In general, cancer incidence and mortality rates are higher, and five-year survival rates lower, in African Americans when compared to the white population. And the situation hasn't changed in 31 years.

In 1963, the five-year cancer survival rate for white Americans was 39 percent, while the rate for blacks was 27 percent, a difference of 12 percent. In 1994, the five-year survival rate was 40 percent for African Americans and 52 percent for whites—a difference of 12 percent.

Examples of disparities for specific cancers include the following:

- **Breast cancer:** the incidence rate in African-American women is 85 percent that of white women (75.2 cases per 100,000 black women vs. 88.8 cases per 100,000 white women), but the number of black women who die from the disease equals the number of white women who die from it (26.9 deaths per 100,000 black women vs. 26.8 deaths per 100,000 white women). If the incidence is lower among African Americans but the mortality is the same as in whites, the survival rate among blacks is lower.

- **Endometrial cancer:** the incidence rate in African-American women is 58 percent that of whites, but mortality among blacks is 67 percent greater than for whites.

- **Bladder cancer:** the incidence rate for blacks is 56 percent that of whites but, again, the number who die is equal: 3.8 per 100,000 in both populations.

- **Cervical cancer:** thanks to the Pap test, which detects this malignancy at an early and treatable stage, the mortality rate from cervical cancer in whites has dropped to 3.2 women per 100,000. The mortality rate for blacks, however, is more than twice as high at 8.7 per 100,000 women. Death rates from cervical cancer are also 30 to 50 percent higher for native Americans, native Hawaiians, and Hispanics.

- **Prostate cancer:** the incidence in African-American men is 61 percent greater than in whites, while the mortality rate is 108 percent that of whites, and the highest in the world.

Why Do These Differences Exist?

The overriding contributor is poverty—a poverty of finances and a poverty of knowledge. Louis Sullivan, president of Morehouse School of Medicine and former U.S. Secretary of Health and Human Services, said that if educational and income levels are taken into account, most of the disparities in cancer mortality between minorities and whites disappears.

Clinically, the major reason for the discrepancies in mortality rates is late diagnosis. For example, a study published in the September 1994 issue of the *Journal of the American Medical Association (JAMA)* compared 612 black and 518 white breast cancer patients. It found that African-American women had more than twice the risk of dying from their tumors as did white women. Much of the difference was due to black women having a more advanced stage of disease at the time of diagnosis.

Often, treatment isn't sought until pain or some other intolerable clinical development finally drives the person to seek medical care, usually at a hospital emergency room. By that time, however, the disease has progressed, and treatment is likely to be of little help.

Late diagnosis is also a leading reason for disparities in cancer mortality between whites and Hispanics, Native Americans, and Asian Americans. Reasons why minorities might receive late diagnosis and treatment include the following:

- The person doesn't recognize cancer symptoms.
- Once symptoms are realized, it takes longer to seek treatment.
- Once treatment is sought, the treatment provided might be less than optimal. There is evidence that subtle racism sometimes results in less-aggressive treatment of minority patients diagnosed at the same stage of disease as white patients. Racism can also come in the form of less-than-sincere attention to a minority patient. How prevalent these problems are remains unknown.
- The person lacks health insurance and, therefore, access to health care. Samuel Broder, former head of the National Cancer Institute once said that "poverty is a carcinogen."
- Mammography or prostate screening facilities are located outside the minority community or are operated by an all-white or nearly all-white staff, which discourages some people from attending.
- Survival priorities and the day-to-day realities of life distract people from seeking preventive health care. Said Harold Freeman, an African American, chairman of the President's Cancer Panel and a member of the National Cancer Advisory Board: "Take a poor woman who is unemployed and has no medical insurance except Medicaid. She has children; maybe she's having difficulty putting

food on the table. She may be afraid of crime in the community. She's told she should have breast examinations, but she's got all these other concerns. She's being told about something that has to do with her future when she's worried about her present." (Freeman is also director of surgery at Harlem Hospital and professor of clinical surgery at Columbia University.)

Cultural differences also present barriers to screenings and health care:

- Language can be a barrier to obtaining health care, particularly for Hispanics and Asian populations.
- Depending on the degree of acculturation, a Hispanic woman might feel the need to have her husband's permission before getting a mammogram or Pap test. If the husband opposes health screening, the woman is likely to remain untested.
- Some individuals think that cancer is incurable and that getting the disease is God's will, so they do not seek care.
- Some Asian Americans view doctors as a last resort and postpone seeking care.

Suggestions for conducting successful public education and screening programs in ethnic communities include the following:

- Involve credible community leaders early when planning a program—local clergy, community workers, Boys' Club directors, YMCA and YWCA leaders, and scout groups, for example.
- Hold focus groups with church and civic leaders or in the community for feedback on how the program will be perceived and how it might be improved.
- Keep advertising tightly focused. Use familiar faces from the ethnic group being targeted in all television, radio, and print ads. Ads for a breast cancer screening program aimed at Hispanics should use Hispanic actors or spokespeople; programs targeted to African Americans should use African Americans. For tips on advertising, study the alcohol and tobacco ads that target ethnic community. For example, a popular Japanese cigarette, Mild 7, is advertised in the U.S. with the slogan: "Made by Asians for Asians."
- Conduct screenings at convenient locations within the ethnic community itself. Include minority physicians and nurses when possible. Provide a person from the community to explain what is to take place during the screening.
- Provide a translator for programs aimed at Hispanics and Asian Americans. This could be a volunteer identified with the help of the community leaders involved in planning the program. Often, the children in a family will speak English while the parent seeking medical treatment does not. But asking the children to translate for

their parents should be avoided when possible. It may be embarrassing and culturally difficult for parents to reveal this personal information through their children.
- Provide aggressive public education campaigns designed with the cultural and ethnic sensitivities in mind.
- Include minorities in clinical trials to help identify ethnic differences in tumor development and response to treatment.

Some research indicates that there might be ethnic differences in cancer susceptibility. This might be due to biological differences between ethnic groups in the way that carcinogens are metabolized. The *JAMA* breast cancer study cited above noted that African-American women were more likely to have breast tumors that were poorly differentiated and lacked estrogen receptors. Both are characteristic of tumors that respond poorly to treatment.

Other research has shown that African-American men appear to have twice the relative risk of developing lung cancer as do whites smoking the same number of cigarettes. Why this is the case is unknown, but it might suggest that African Americans and whites metabolize tobacco carcinogens differently.

Nonetheless, experts such as Sullivan and Freeman agree that improvements in socioeconomic status, and early diagnosis and treatment will eliminate most ethnic disparities in cancer mortality.

Gene Control/Gene Regulation

Gene control and gene regulation refer to the way genes are turned on and off in the cell. This, in turn, controls activity—including cell growth and division—within the cell. Gene mutations can interfere with that control and lead to uncontrolled cell growth and cancer.

Most cells in the body contain a complete set of 46 chromosomes. Yet, a nerve cell is not a bone cell is not a muscle cell. Why not? Because different genes are active in different cells.

A gene is a length of DNA that contains the instructions for a protein. A portion of this DNA serves as a switch. This is the regulatory region of the gene. The switch turns the gene on or off—that is, increases or decreases its activity. (The region of a gene that codes for the protein itself is the structural region. This is the part of the gene that is copied as mRNA [see "Genes, Mutations, and Chromosomes," page 40; and "Proteins and Protein Synthesis," page 66].)

What is it that flips this gene switch? Proteins known as regulatory proteins. These attach, or bind, to the DNA at the proper site on the DNA to activate or repress gene activity. Regulatory proteins are produced by still other genes that themselves are activated by chemical messengers such as hormones and growth factors.

Through gene regulation, genes are turned on when their proteins are needed and turned off when their proteins are not needed. Some genes are always active; others are turned on only at certain stages of life; and still others may be turned on and off repeatedly during life.

Cell division is also under gene control. Cells prepare to divide by producing the protein cyclin. For this to occur, the gene for cyclin must be activated by a hormone or growth factor. The cyclin then binds to another protein, cdc2, and that, in turn, activates a series of enzymes that results in cell division.

Genes, Mutations, and Chromosomes

A gene is a length of DNA that contains the instructions needed by the cell to make a protein. A chromosome is a contiguous string of genes. Mutations are flaws that occur in genes.

Genes

Human beings have about 100,000 genes in the 23 chromosomes found in a normal egg or sperm. Upon conception, and a million billion (10^{15}) cell divisions later, the descendants of those original genes reside in each body cell of an adult—a remarkable job of biological photocopying!

Genes come in different sizes. Some are composed of long lengths of DNA, others are relatively short. For example, the *myc* gene, which plays an important role in a variety of cancers, is a small gene—it consists of a length of DNA made up of about 5,000 base pairs (i.e., 5,000 ladder rungs on the DNA helix). It codes for a protein that regulates cell division.

Structure of a gene: A gene has two main regions (Fig. 3). One functions as a switch that turns the gene on or off. This is the regulatory region (see "Gene Control/Gene Regulation," page 39).

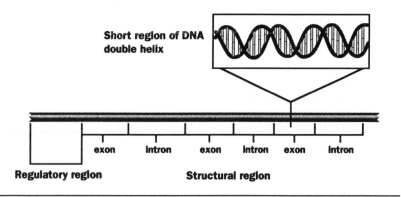

Short region of DNA double helix

Regulatory region

exon intron exon intron exon intron

Structural region

Figure 3. A small gene showing the regulatory and structural regions. The structural region is divided into introns and exons.

The second region—the structural region—contains the information that describes the structure of the protein the gene is responsible for. The structural region of the gene is itself divided into segments known as exons that are separated from one another by segments known as introns.

Exons contain the actual genetic information that describes the structure of the protein. Introns are sometimes involved in gene regulation, but in most cases their function isn't known. The *myc* gene, for example, consists of only three exons. Large genes may have 30 or more exons. During protein synthesis, both exons and introns are copied as messenger RNA, but the introns are edited out before the mRNA leaves the nucleus (see "Proteins and Protein Synthesis," page 66).

Function of a gene: Genes have two fundamental roles in life:

- In body cells, genes control the production of proteins or parts of proteins. Flawed—or mutated—genes in a body cell may be harmless, may remain hidden, may be fatal to the cell or lead to cancer, but they will not be passed along to offspring.
- In eggs and sperm, genes are the basic units of heredity. Through the genes in the germ cells, genetic traits—including any mutations—are passed along to children.

Mutations

Mutations are flaws that occur in genes. Genetic mutations are rare events. The natural average mutation rate is about one mutation per million cell divisions. Gene mutations can be one of the following:

- An addition mutation—one or more bases (building blocks of DNA) is added to the makeup of the gene.
- A deletion mutation—one or more bases is lost from the gene.
- A substitution mutation—one base is substituted for another in the gene.

Gene mutations are thought to be the fundamental cause of cancer. They can occur spontaneously or can be caused by physical, chemical, or viral carcinogens. (Occasionally, a mutation benefits an animal or plant in a way that helps it survive better than others of their species. This can advance its evolutionary progression.)

Chromosomes

A chromosome is one long molecule of DNA plus a variety of associated proteins. Most cells in the human body contain 46 chromosomes, all of which are highly condensed to enable them to fit into the cell nucleus (Fig. 4). It's much like fitting 10,000 miles of string into an average-sized room, said Dennis Ross in his *Introduction to Molecular Medicine* (1992).

The 46 chromosomes consist of 23 pairs, with one set coming from the mother and one from the father. Except for the X and Y chromosomes in a male, the members of pairs appear identical under the microscope. To view them, the chromosomes must be in their most highly condensed state during cell division and specially stained. One way to check chromosomes for defects is to photograph them through the microscope and compare the members of a pair, a process known as karyotyping.

The sex cells—eggs and sperm—carry only 23 chromosomes. When a sperm fertilizes an egg, the embryo then has the normal complement of 46 chromosomes. Eggs and sperm are also referred to as gametes and as germ cells. (Other cells in the body are known as somatic cells.) The genes in germ cells are collectively referred to as the "germ line."

Defects in chromosomes usually have severe consequences. They can lead to spontaneous abortion, birth defects, and, sometimes, cancer. Chromosome defects include the following:

- Deletions—a segment of a chromosome (i.e., a sequence of genes) is lost through viral attack, radiation exposure, or chemical action.
- Duplications—a sequence of genes is repeated.
- Inversions—a sequence of genes is separated from a chromosome and is then reinserted in the same place, but backward. This changes the relative order of the genes on the chromosome.
- Translocations—part of one chromosome breaks free and attaches to another chromosome other than its mate. In Burkitt's lymphoma, for example, a segment of chromosome 8 is transferred to chromosome 14. This leads to abnormal activity of the *myc* gene, which is located on chromosome 8, and cancer. What was a normal *myc* gene is now a *myc* oncogene.

Figure 4 (opposite). The organization of DNA in a chromosome. 1. An entire chromosome, condensed, as it would be during mitosis. 2. The arms of a chromosome are coiled (in reality, they are tightly coiled). 3. A cross section of the strand making up the coil shows it is made up of loops of DNA (plus proteins) anchored to a protein scaffolding within the strand (the loops would actually be extremely long and thin). 4. A cross-section of one of the loops shows that it is made up of tablet-like structures known as nucleosomes. 5. Individual nucleosomes consist of two turns of the DNA helix wrapped around globular histone proteins. 6. A short region of the DNA double helix.

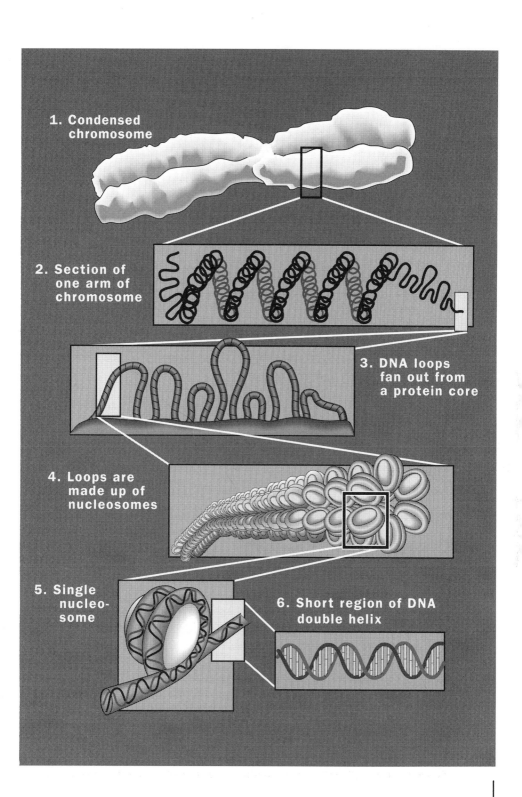

1. Condensed chromosome

2. Section of one arm of chromosome

3. DNA loops fan out from a protein core

4. Loops are made up of nucleosomes

5. Single nucleosome

6. Short region of DNA double helix

Heredity and Cancer

Heredity can play an important role in cancer in three different ways. Some cancers have been linked to specific genes; these are hereditary cancers. Some cancers have not been linked to specific genes, but they sometimes occur in families at a higher-than-expected rate; these are said to be familial. In addition, cancer may occur in one person rather than another because of the normal genetic differences that exist between individuals; for example, some people may be born with enzyme systems that more effectively repair the genetic damage that leads to cancer.

Note that having several cases of cancer in a family does not mean the disease was inherited or is familial. One in four Americans is likely to be stricken with cancer during his or her life, so cancer can arise in several members of a family and heredity need not be involved at all.

Also, the occurrence of hereditary and familial cancers is likely to be greatest among first- and second-degree relatives. First-degree relatives are those that share half your genes (mother, father, sister, brother, children). Second-degree relatives share a quarter of your genes (grandparents, aunts, uncles).

Cancers Linked to Specific Genes

A number of cancers are hereditary in the classic sense—they are linked to a specific gene that may (but not necessarily) be passed from parent to offspring.

- Breast cancer: heredity is thought to be responsible for 5 percent of all breast cancer cases. A family history of breast cancer increases the risk two to four times. An estimated 15 to 20 percent of breast cancer is thought to be familial.
- Colorectal cancer: 16 percent of colorectal cancers are thought to be due to heredity. Familial polyposis of the colon (FPC) is the most clearly hereditary condition that predisposes a person to cancer; it accounts for about 1 percent of cases. (FPC begins with thousands of polyps developing in the colon. These individuals are almost 100 percent certain of developing colon cancer by age 50).

Less common inherited cancers include retinoblastoma, endocrine tumors, and certain types of skin cancers.

Cancer is also associated with a number of genetic disorders, including Down syndrome (leukemia) and Klinefelter's syndrome (mediastinal teratoma).

In addition, more than 200 disorders resulting from the mutation of a single gene involve the development of tumors.

Familial Cancers

Familial cancers arise with unusually high frequency within families, but the pattern of occurrence doesn't follow the classic rules of genetic inheritance.

- Ovarian cancer: about 5 percent of cases are thought to be familial.
- Lung cancer: if a first-degree relative develops lung cancer, your risk of developing the disease is three times greater than that of someone in the general population.
- Endometrial cancer: 1 to 2 percent of cases are thought to be familial.
- Melanoma: a history of melanoma in a family increases risk two to eight times.
- Prostate cancer: a man's risk of developing prostate cancer is doubled if he has first-degree male relatives with the disease.

Cancer Susceptibility and Heredity

Normal genetic differences between individuals may leave some people more susceptible to cancer for indirect reasons. Some people may develop cancer because they have a system of enzymes that works a little less effectively than in most people. Such enzyme systems are used to detoxify carcinogens, for example, or to repair DNA damaged by a carcinogen.

Heredity or normal genetic differences may make it more difficult to treat some cancers. The drug mitomycin-C, for example, is used to treat superficial bladder cancer. But the drug works in only about half of patients, and currently there is no way to predict who it will help and who it won't. For mitomycin-C to work, it must be activated by two enzymes in cells. It is thought that some people lack the genes for these enzymes. Mitomycin-C wouldn't work in these patients no matter how much was given. Researchers are testing this hypothesis. If it is true, people with bladder cancer could be tested for the presence of these genes, thereby helping to determine if treatment with mitomycin-C is appropriate.

Hormones and Cancer

The development of four major cancers—breast, endometrial, ovarian, and prostate—is affected by hormones in the body. Both breast and uterine tissues are targets of the steroid hormone estrogen. One of the actions of estrogen is to stimulate cell production such as growth of breast epithelial cells. One way it does this is by triggering the release of growth factors, chemicals that trigger cell division. Researchers suspect estrogen may also promote tumor growth in the same way.

Breast cancer: There are two major types of breast cancer: hormone dependent and hormone independent. In hormone-dependent breast cancer, the tumor cells have estrogen receptors (ER positive tumors) and need estrogen to grow. In hormone-independent breast cancer, the cells lack estrogen receptors (ER negative tumors) and estrogen is not required for tumor growth.

Whether a tumor is ER positive or ER negative is important in determining how to treat the tumor. ER positive tumors are often treated using anti-hormone therapy. An important example is the anti-estrogen drug tamoxifen. Such drugs—known as estrogen antagonists—attach to estrogen receptors, thereby blocking them so that they can't be triggered by the estrogen produced by the body. An experimental therapy for breast cancer uses drugs to block an enzyme—aromatase—that is key to the production of estrogen by cells. The drugs, aromatase inhibitors, are undergoing clinical testing in Europe and England, and trials may soon begin in the U.S. ER negative tumors tend to be more aggressive and difficult to treat.

Endometrial cancer: Like the breast, the uterus is a target of estrogen, progesterone, and other steroid hormones. Endometrial tumors often have receptors for the hormone progesterone (PR positive tumors). Advanced PR positive tumors respond somewhat to treatment with progesterone. Endometrial tumors lacking the receptor (PR negative tumors) are unlikely to respond to progesterone treatment. Ironically, tamoxifen, which is used to treat breast cancer, increases the risk of endometrial cancer.

Ovarian cancer: Estrogen reduces the risk of ovarian cancer. Women who take oral contraceptives for six or more years, for example, have a 40 percent lower risk of developing the disease compared to the general population (0.6 risk compared to a relative risk of 1.0 for the general population).

Prostate cancer: The growth of prostate cancer is aided by male hormones, which as a group are called androgens. Anti-hormone therapy is used to slow the growth of metastatic prostate cancer. Anti-hormone therapy includes suppressing the release of male hormones using high doses of female hormones (estrogens), hormone-suppressing drugs, and anti-androgens to block androgen receptors. Or the testicles are removed to eliminate the major source of androgens. If prostate cancer is confined to the prostate, surgical removal of the gland or radiotherapy is usually the best treatment.

Hospice and Cancer

Hospice programs provide physical and emotional support for patients in the final phase of life-limiting illnesses and for their families. Of the people in hospice programs, 84 percent are cancer patients.

"Hospice" also describes a philosophy. The hospice philosophy recognizes that the end of life is a part of life. That it is a unique time of growth and development—a time of healing, forgiveness, contemplation, and preparation. A time to make peace and feel at peace. A time for good-byes.

This time of growth requires that the patient have quality of life, that he or she be comfortable, and free from chronic, severe pain. Hospice programs accomplish this through aggressive, around-the-clock pain and symptom control. Every effort is made to keep the patient alert and in touch with loved ones.

Hospice programs provide interdisciplinary care. It can include physicians, nurses, social workers, chaplains, home health aides, counselors, and volunteers. This care can be administered in the home or sometimes in a hospice center, which provides a home-like setting. Patients receiving treatment that attempts to cure their disease are not eligible for hospice care. Hospice care is usually covered by insurance, but it is also provided without regard for ability to pay. Bereavement counseling is provided to families.

Hospice programs accept patients who, in the judgment of the patient's personal physician and a hospice physician, have six months or less to live. Unfortunately, may people who could benefit from hospice are referred to the program during the last couple of weeks of life, too late to take advantage of all that hospice has to offer.

When should physicians and patients discuss hospice care? Bernice Wilson, executive director of the Ohio Hospice Organization, offered this suggestion: "When the physical, psychological, spiritual, and financial burdens of curative care seem to outweigh the benefits, that's when the patient should seek referral to hospice."

To locate hospice programs in your community, look under "Hospices" in the yellow pages or call the national Hospice Hotline at 1-800-658-8898 for referrals and general hospice information.

Identifying Carcinogens

Identifying chemicals, substances, and mixtures that cause cancer in animals or humans—that are carcinogens—ordinarily requires several kinds of evidence.

Carcinogen testing affects many industries, including the producers and developers of consumer products, industrial chemicals, pesticides, pharmaceuticals, and agricultural and food products. Such companies must prove to federal and state regulatory agencies that new products are safe for use or consumption by humans. Test results are also used to regulate exposure to substances in the workplace. In addition to testing of a final product, testing must be done on substances that occur as intermediates in the production of a chemical.

The results of carcinogen tests are given to the regulatory agencies that oversee a particular industry as evidence that the chemical is safe for use. These agencies include the Food and Drug Administration (FDA), the Consumer Products Safety Commission, the Occupational Safety and Health Administration (OSHA), and the Environmental Protection Agency (EPA).

The National Toxicology Program (NTP), a division of the National Institute of Environmental Health Sciences, is responsible for carcinogenicity testing of all chemicals present in the environment as of 1977. The chemical and pharmaceutical industries are responsible for carcinogenicity testing of all chemicals released into the environment since 1977. The NTP monitors these data along with other regulatory agencies.

Another important agency that evaluates the carcinogenic risk of chemicals is the International Agency for Research on Cancer (IARC), an arm of the World Health Organization. The agency publishes monographs that evaluate the epidemiologic and laboratory evidence of the cancer-causing hazard posed by individual chemicals and mixtures of chemicals.

Evidence that a chemical, substance, or mixture causes cancer in animals or humans is obtained using the following kinds of studies:

• Examination of the chemical structure and physical properties of the substance.

- Tests that use bacteria or cells grown in the laboratory.
- Short-term animal tests.
- Long-term (chronic) animal tests.
- Human epidemiologic studies.

The first three kinds of studies provide preliminary or suggestive evidence that a compound may be carcinogenic; long-term animal tests and epidemiological studies are considered the strongest evidence that a chemical, substance, or mixture causes cancer in humans.

Molecular structure or physical properties of a substance: If the molecular structure of a substance closely resembles the structure of a known carcinogen, there is a good possibility that the substance being studied will also be carcinogenic.

Bacterial tests and tests using cultured cells: Usually, the molecular structure of a chemical gives little clue about its potential to cause cancer. In many cases, once a chemical is in the body it undergoes metabolic activation; i.e., it is converted first to one then to other intermediate chemicals. It is one or more of these intermediate chemicals that damages DNA—that is carcinogenic. The chain of chemical reactions is the activation pathway. Often there is no way to predict whether the activation pathway for a chemical will lead to formation of a carcinogen. So researchers next subject the chemical to relatively quick and inexpensive bacterial or cell assay tests, of which there are more than 100. These tests reveal whether the chemical damages DNA, kills bacteria that lack DNA repair systems, damages chromosomes, or transforms cells to cancer cells.

The results of these tests provide an early measure of carcinogenicity, although they do not alone determine whether a chemical is carcinogenic in whole animals. On the other hand, if the chemical is similar in structure to a known carcinogen, and it causes genetic damage in bacterial or cell tests, a consumer products company is likely to halt its further development unless it is a life-saving compound.

Short-term animal tests: These tests expose rodents to the chemical for periods of months. The tests use special strains of rodents that develop tumors of the lung, liver, skin, or other tissue more readily than other strains. The experiments use at least three groups of animals, two of which are exposed to at least two doses of the chemical, while the other serves as a control. Often, the control animals develop tumors spontaneously, but these tests can still show a valid difference if the number of tumors is significantly greater in the exposed versus the control groups, and tumor development is shown to depend on the dose (i.e., the number of tumors is lower in animals exposed to the lower dose of chemical).

Long-term, or chronic, animal tests: The long-term test developed by the NTP is considered to be the "gold standard" for determining whether a chemical or substance is a likely to cause cancer in humans.

The chronic bioassay is run for a period of two years. The test itself involves exposing two species of animals—usually particular strains of rats and mice—to the chemical. Equal numbers of males and females are used, and the animals are exposed to three concentrations of the chemical. A fourth group of animals is not exposed to the chemical; they serve as the comparison—or control—group.

The NTP chronic bioassay typically uses 400 animals: 50 males and 50 females at each of three concentrations of the chemical, plus 100 controls. The test chemical is administered in food or water, or it is delivered to the stomach through a tube.

If more cancers occur in the exposed animals than in the control animals, and if statistical tests show that the difference is significant, then the chemical is judged to be an animal carcinogen—and a probable human carcinogen. This judgment is based on finding more cancers overall or in one or more organ sites.

At the end of the test, a board-certified veterinary pathologist or a medical pathologist examines virtually all the tissues in the animals for both large and microscopic tumors. Even the blood and urine of the animals are scrutinized. The NTP chronic bioassay is expensive: evaluating a single chemical costs $1 million to $1.5 million.

Since passage of the Toxic Substances Control Act in 1977, food products companies, pharmaceutical and chemical manufacturing firms, and many consumer products companies have also used the two-year rodent bioassay to test the safety of new chemicals and additives before introducing them to consumers.

Epidemiological studies: Epidemiology studies link the incidence of a disease in humans to a risk factor in the environment. They are currently the only certain way to determine whether a chemical that causes cancer in rats and mice also causes cancer in humans. In fact, epidemiological evidence often identifies a possible carcinogen first, followed by laboratory research designed to confirm the possible association. Epidemiologic evidence established the link between smoking and cancer, and identified such workplace-related cancers as those caused by asbestos and vinyl chloride.

But there are limits to epidemiologic studies. Tobacco, asbestos, and vinyl chloride came to the attention of researchers because they caused rare cancers. Lung cancer was rare before the mass production of cigarettes; asbestos causes mesothelioma, a rare tumor of the lining of the chest cavity; and vinyl chloride produces hemangiosarcoma, a rare malignancy arising from blood vessels. Chemicals that increase the risk of common cancers are difficult to identify through epidemiological studies. A chemical that causes a 5 to 10 percent increase in colon cancer, for example, would take a massive epidemiological study to detect. Hence, the need remains for laboratory and animal tests that identify possible carcinogens.

Do the Results of Animal Tests Apply to Humans?

Many scientists in government, industry, and academic research debate the usefulness of chronic bioassays. The debate focuses on the use of the maximum tolerated dose (MTD) in animal studies. The MTD is the highest of the three doses of chemical that animals are exposed to during short-term and long-term assays.

MTD is defined as the maximum amount of chemical that can be fed to the animals without making them sick, causing them to lose more than 10 percent of their weight, or shortening their life span from effects other than cancer. The MTD is estimated by giving rodents a lethal amount of the chemical, then dropping that dose back a little. The other dosages used in two-year tests are usually one-half and one-fifth the MTD. In many cases, however, the MTD is thousands of times greater than the proportional dose to which humans would ever be exposed under normal conditions.

So why use the MTD? One reason is that the test has to produce cancer in enough animals to demonstrate a statistical association between the chemical and the disease. That is, scientists must be sure that the tumors didn't occur by chance alone. Even though cancer is the second leading killer of Americans, it is still a relatively rare event; a common cancer such as breast cancer, for example, actually strikes only 2 percent of 50-year-old women nationally. Animal tests, however, must show an effect using only 50 animals that have a relatively short life span. In fact, even the most potent of known human carcinogens must be given at high doses to produce cancer in animals.

Many scientists feel that in most cases the MTD overwhelms an animal's normal physiological or biochemical defenses against cancer, thereby predisposing them to develop the disease. They believe it might be appropriate for testing chemicals that involve exposure to huge doses—such as medicinal drugs or exposure chemicals in the workplace; but it is not appropriate for judging the effects of exposure to traces of chemicals in the environment.

Furthermore, proper regulation of a chemical may require more than showing that exposure to the chemical causes cancer in animals: we must also know *how* it causes cancer. Saccharin is one example. In the late 1970s, saccharin was labeled a carcinogen because it caused bladder cancer in rats. More recent research has shown that tumors were caused by crystals that formed in the rat bladder. The crystals scratch the bladder wall, killing cells. The death of these cells causes others to divide. This constant cell killing and cell division leads to cancer. Crystal formation doesn't occur when saccharin is present at a low dose, which indicates that the sweetener should be safe to consume at a low dose. (During the animal tests, saccharin made up 7.5 percent of the animals' diet—equivalent to 800 diet sodas per day in humans.)

There are other problems in applying the results of animal tests to humans. For example, the cells in a rat or mouse often do not process—metabolize—a particular chemical in the same way that cells in the human body do. (Rats, in fact, can metabolize some chemicals differently than do mice). How a chemical affects animals, therefore, is only a best guess, an approximation, of how the chemical might affect humans. Proponents of the chronic test point out, however, that every chemical known to be carcinogenic in humans is also carcinogenic in animals.

Immunotherapy and Cancer Vaccines

Immunotherapy is the use of the immune system to kill tumor cells. Immunotherapy has taken a place along with surgery, radiation therapy, and chemotherapy as an accepted treatment for many cancers. This progress became possible only after the discovery of cytokines, lymphokines, and growth factors, and it became practical only after recombinant DNA technology made it possible to produce these biologic substances in large quantities. Most immunotherapy treatments are experimental and are conducted through clinical trials. Often, a key objective in immunotherapy is to trick the immune system into recognizing a tumor as foreign tissue.

Active Immunotherapy

Active immunotherapy involves stimulating the patient's own immune system to actively attack tumor cells. This is accomplished using a variety of substances, including interferon (IFN), interleukin (IL), tumor necrosis factor (TNF), and injections of antibodies or tumor antigens.

Cancer vaccines use antibodies or tumor antigens to stimulate the body's immune response to the tumor. One cancer vaccine, for example, contains the protein beta-HCG (human chorionic gonadotropin). This protein occurs in the placenta during pregnancy (its presence in urine is the basis for pregnancy tests) and on tumor cells. A cancer patient is given HCG that is attached to disabled diphtheria toxin. The disabled diphtheria toxin (a diphtheria toxoid) stimulates a response from the immune system, which forms antibodies against HCG. The antibodies can then act against the tumor cells.

Passive and Adoptive Immunotherapy

The term "passive" is used because the patient's immune system is not being directly activated. One form of passive immunotherapy is monoclonal antibody therapy. It uses monoclonal antibodies to attract cancer-fighting cells to the tumor or to deliver a toxin to the tumor.

Adoptive immunotherapy involves removing lymphocytes from the patient, boosting their anti-cancer activity, growing them in large numbers, then returning them to the patient.

LAK cells: Initial experiments in adoptive immunotherapy involved removing lymphocytes from the blood of a patient and growing them in the presence of the lymphokine interleukin-2 (IL-2), an immune stimulator. The cells were then returned to the patient. These lymphocytes were called lymphokine-activated killer (LAK) cells.

TILs: A stronger response against tumor cells is obtained using lymphocytes isolated from the tumor itself. These tumor-infiltrating lymphocytes (TILs) are grown in the presence of IL-2 and returned to the body to attack the tumor. Researchers are also using radiolabeled monoclonal antibodies for tumor antigens to even more closely identify lymphocytes specific for tumor cells.

Gene therapy: This involves isolating immune system cells from a patient and boosting their tumor-destroying action by transplanting into them a gene for a cancer-killing cytokine such as TNF. The transformed cells are then grown to large numbers and returned to the patient.

Metastasis

Metastasis is the spread or movement of cancer cells from the primary cancer site to another area of the body. Other than certain white blood cells, this is something most normal cells cannot do, and it is the most deadly characteristic of cancer.

During metastasis, tumor cells penetrate the fibrous boundaries that normally separate one tissue from another. The tumor can also infiltrate the walls of blood or lymph vessels and shed cancer cells into the circulation. In the blood, these tumor cells are carried downstream to become lodged in the next capillary bed. Tumor cells shed from colon cancer, for example, are carried by the circulation to the liver, where secondary tumors then arise. Tumor cells from other areas of the body can be carried by the blood through the heart and on to the lungs, where they start metastatic lung tumors. Tumor cells shed into the lymph system often establish themselves in the nearest cluster of lymph nodes, where they grow before spreading to more distant parts of the body. Fewer than 1 in 10,000 cells shed from the primary tumor are thought to survive, but these are enough to spawn secondary tumors elsewhere in the body.

About 30 percent of new patients with solid tumors have detectable metastases. About half the remaining patients will be cured by treating the tumor alone; the remainder will have undetectable metastases that will eventually develop into tumors. Tumor staging includes a measure of whether a malignancy has spread beyond the primary tumor. This is a major factor in determining a patient's prognosis.

The goal of early detection is to remove the primary tumor before metastasis has occurred. Unfortunately, some tumors apparently metastasize before they are large enough to be found. The spread of such micrometastases may explain why many women die of breast cancer even after early detection of their primary tumors.

Scientists have recently learned that metastasis can occur only after certain genes are turned on. These genes produce the enzymes necessary for the cancer cells to penetrate other tissues and invade blood vessel walls. These enzymes, and receptors for these enzymes, may provide targets for new drugs that can block the process of metastasis.

Oncogenes

The Walt Disney film *Fantasia* includes a segment called "The Sorcerer's Apprentice." The apprentice is a quiet, mild-mannered fellow who is supposed to sweep the floor, carry water, and keep order around the sorcerer's laboratory. At one point, the apprentice dons the wizard's pointed hat, casts a spell on a broom, and commands it to carry water for him. In the end, the spell causes the broom to multiply out of control, overwhelming the apprentice and nearly destroying the laboratory.

Something similar happens when a mutation produces an oncogene. Oncogenes are normal genes that have gone awry because of a mutation or chromosome defect that arises following exposure to carcinogens (see "Carcinogenesis," page 6).

Like the sorcerer's apprentice who used his broom to help keep order in the lab, these genes produce proteins that normally maintain order in the cell. They play critical roles in regulating cell growth, cell division, and cell differentiation. Exposure to carcinogens, however, can damage these genes. Mutations and chromosomal defects accumulate, casting a metaphorical spell that causes the genes to become hyperactive and overproduce their proteins. At that point, the normal genes have become oncogenes. In theory, the cells with the mutated genes then multiply out of control and overwhelm the body, resulting in cancer.

Most oncogenes fall into one of a handful of main groups. Each group represents a step in the chain of command that leads to cell division. Taken together, they are known as the signal transduction pathway. They are steps through which a chemical signal arriving at the surface of the cell can be passed to the interior of the cell and activate one or more genes. The action of those genes, through the proteins they produce, can then trigger cell division. In a simplified way, the pathway works as follows (see Fig. 5):

1. A primary messenger—a growth factor, for example—arrives at the cell surface signaling that it is time to divide.

2. The growth factor binds to a receptor molecule on the cell surface. The receptor molecule conveys the signal from the outside surface of the cell membrane to the inside surface.

3. On the inside surface of the membrane, the receptor activates a second messenger. In fact, the signal passes through the cell cytoplasm along a chain of two, three, or more secondary messengers. These can include cAMP (cyclic adenosine monophosphate) and a class of proteins known as G proteins.

4. The signal eventually passes to a protein kinase, a class of enzymes that energizes other molecules.

5. The kinase moves into the nucleus, where it activates a protein, a transcription factor. Transcription factors, also known as DNA-binding proteins, bind to DNA and turn on one gene or a set of genes.

Genes for any of the components making up the pathway could become oncogenes if mutated. For example, a mutated growth-factor gene could result in overproduction of the primary messenger and lead to runaway cell division. The same could be happen through overproduction of cell-surface receptor proteins, second messengers, protein kinases, and transcription factors.

Some Oncogenes and Their Role in the Signal Transduction Pathway

Step	Oncogene protein	Oncogene
Primary messenger	Platelet-derived growth factor	c-*sis*
Receptor	Growth-factor receptors	c-*erbB* c-*fms* c-*kit*
Second messenger	G proteins	c-*ras*
Protein kinases		c-*mos* c-*raf* c-*abl* *src*
Transcription factors		c-*myc* c-*fos* c-*jun*

Figure 5 (opposite). The signal transduction pathway. This theoretical concept explains how a hormone or growth factor can bind to a receptor on the surface of the cell and activate genes in the cell's nucleus. When mutated, the genes coding for proteins making up the pathway might also be considered oncogenes because mutations in these genes could lead to a loss in control of cell growth and possibly cancer.

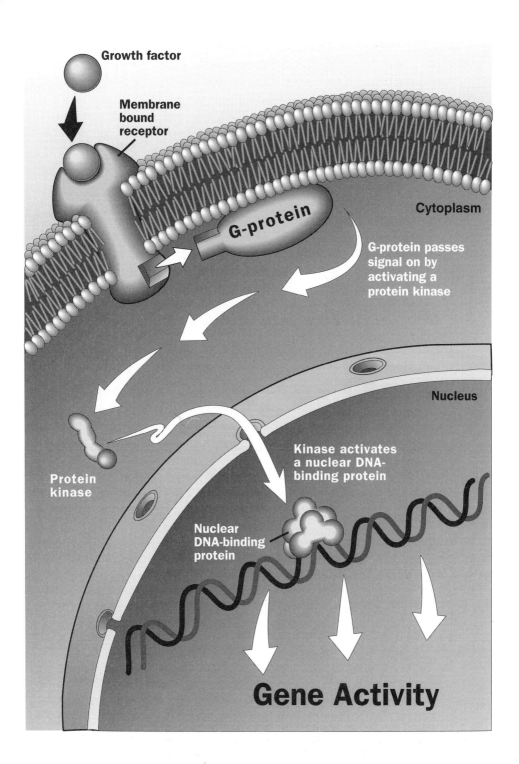

Growth factor

Membrane bound receptor

G-protein

Cytoplasm

G-protein passes signal on by activating a protein kinase

Nucleus

Kinase activates a nuclear DNA-binding protein

Protein kinase

Nuclear DNA-binding protein

Gene Activity

More than 100 oncogenes have been discovered so far.

Note, however, that human cancers are thought to develop only after a number of mutations produce several oncogenes. Furthermore, this must be accompanied by mutations that disable a second group of regulatory genes, tumor suppressor genes (see page 78). In most cases, this probably requires constant, long-term exposure to carcinogens. At the same time, the cell is attempting to repair mutations as they occur. Sometimes it does so successfully, and sometimes it doesn't. This requirement for a number of mutations in specific genes, with the cell racing to repair the damage, is thought to explain why cancer can take years to develop.

Pain Control and Cancer

"Pain is more than the hurt," said a patient with advanced prostate cancer. It means fatigue, weakness, weariness, and weight loss. "It extracts a price and you don't realize it's happening. Pain just beats you up."

Pain is one of the most feared symptoms of cancer; it can be persistent and debilitating. A third of all patients undergoing treatment for cancer suffer moderate to severe pain, as do 60 to 90 percent of patients with metastatic cancer. Some 15 percent of patients with non-metastatic disease also experience long-term pain. About 65 to 70 percent of chronic cancer pain is caused directly by the tumor; 25 to 30 percent is due to anti-cancer therapy; up to 10 percent is not associated with either the tumor or the treatment.

Pain is also one of the most under-treated symptoms of cancer—about 60 percent of patients who experience pain could be receiving better treatment for it. The problem has received national attention in recent years, and in 1994 the U.S. Department of Health and Human Services issued guidelines for cancer pain control.

Patients can experience acute, chronic, and break-through pain.

- Acute pain occurs suddenly and has a short duration. It can be caused by the tumor or by the treatment for the tumor.
- Chronic pain is pain that persists for a long period of time. It can cause changes in personality, lifestyle, and ability to function. Treatment of chronic pain is often complex. It involves treatment of the pain and of its psychological and social side effects. Chronic pain can be tumor-related or treatment related. Treatment-related pain arises, for example, in patients who have had a limb amputated and experience phantom limb pain. This is pain that seems to arise in the limb that has been removed. Some types of chemotherapy cause neuropathy by killing or damaging nerve fibers. This produces burning pain that can persist for months to years until nerve function returns.
- Break-through pain occurs in patients receiving continuous pain treatment that adequately controls chronic pain. It is an intense acute pain that "breaks through" this continuous treatment. Patients are given a second, short-duration medication to take when break-

through pain occurs (this can happen several times a day, and accompany certain activities).

Cancer causes pain in a number of ways. A tumor can inflame mucous membranes or surrounding tissues, causing pain. A malignancy that invades bone weakens the bone, causing it to develop fractures that produce pain. A tumor that invades the spinal column can transform a strong vertebra into a jelly-like mass, causing it to collapse. This compresses nerves and causes pain. A tumor growing in the bowel can cause an obstruction and intense pain. Rapidly growing tumors can outpace their blood supply, causing tumor cells to die. This release toxins into the blood that can cause pain.

Treatment of cancer pain involves the use of three groups of drugs:

- Aspirin and other non-steroidal anti-inflammatory drugs (some of which are prescription drugs), and acetominophen.
- Opioid pain relievers such as codeine, morphine, morphine derivatives, sentanyl, and methadone. Opioids are the drugs of choice for controlling moderate to severe cancer pain.
- Adjuvant analgesic (pain-killing) agents. These include anti-inflammatory steroids; tricyclic antidepressants, which improve the ability to sleep and increase the power of opioid drugs; and amphetamines, which decrease sedation and increase the power of opioids.

To determine what drug and dosage to use, physicians look to an "analgesic ladder" developed by the World Health Organization. Treatment of mild pain begins with the use of aspirin or other non-steroidal anti-inflammatory drugs; for severe pain, treatment begins with opioids, possibly combined with non-steroidal anti-inflammatory drugs given by mouth.

Treatment of severe pain may involve use of high doses of opioid drugs such as oral morphine or methadone. For persistent cancer pain, the drugs should be taken around the clock and "as needed" for breakthrough pain. But if the pain is too great, the dose required to control it becomes too high. The patient becomes lethargic and mildly sedated, which affects quality of life. Other side effects can include constipation, forgetfulness, loss of memory, inability to concentrate, and itching.

For patients who cannot take oral medication or for whom the dose of opioids becomes too high, pain control is achieved by administering the drug intravenously or by using a sentanyl skin patch. Another alternative is delivering the drug directly to the spinal cord through a catheter. The catheter is attached to a small pump that can be worn externally or implanted in the patient's abdomen. Given this way, the dose needed for pain relief can be as little as 1 percent of that needed in a tablet, and the side effects of the opioids are greatly decreased. Break-through pain is then controlled using a second drug such as liquid morphine.

Radiation therapy is also sometimes used to relieve pain by shrinking the size of tumors.

Last, it's important to note that treatment of cancer pain often does not eliminate pain entirely: it brings it down to a tolerable level. To cope with the pain that remains, patients rely on biofeedback, massage, listening to music, or pursuing hobbies.

Why is cancer pain relief often inadequate? In part it occurs because many physicians believe that diagnosing and treating pain is a job they can and should do themselves. Yet, most physicians—including oncologists—are not adequately trained to assess and treat severe pain. Pain assessment is not addressed well in most medical schools, and there is as yet no good diagnostic tool for measuring pain. It requires gauging intensity of pain and degree of suffering. This can make pain assessment tricky and time consuming because pain tolerance is different in different people. Patients who are not receiving adequate pain relief should seek a referral to a pain specialist or to a hospital pain service or clinic.

Fear of addiction—drug dependency—prevents many patients from receiving adequate pain relief. The fear exists among physicians and families alike. Some physicians fear that prescribing high doses of opioid drugs will make patients drug dependent. And some patients refuse to use drugs such as morphine for fear they will become drug dependent and suffer withdrawal. Sometimes, well-intended family members will even try to talk a patient out of taking the drugs for fear that the patient will become addicted.

In reality, drug dependence and withdrawal rarely occur in pain patients, although they do have to be taken off the drug gradually. But this is also true of steroid drugs prescribed for asthma, inflammation, and other problems.

Pollution of the Environment and Cancer

Pollution of air, water, and land is estimated to account for about 2 percent of human cancer cases.

Some evidence suggests that air pollutants produced by the burning of fossil fuels play a role in causing lung cancer among city dwellers. The prevalence of cigarette smoking, however, makes this assertion difficult to prove. Other environmental pollutants that may cause cancer include airborne arsenic and microscopic asbestos fibers inhaled into the lungs. Chlorofluorocarbon (CFC) pollution, which damages the Earth's ozone layer and allows more ultraviolet light to reach the planet's surface, is expected to cause an increase in skin cancer.

Contamination of groundwater by carcinogenic chemicals such as polychlorobiphenyls (PCBs), dioxin, and carbon tetrachloride, for example, remains an area of concern. The addition of chlorine to surface waters (e.g., shallow wells) to provide clean drinking water is thought to increase cancer risk. The chlorine reacts with organic material in the water to produce chlorinated compounds that are carcinogenic. Prolonged consumption may increase the risk of bladder and colon cancers.

Cancers caused by the use of pesticides and herbicides are of concern to many in the public. In the early 1980s, the U.S. Department of the Interior banned the use of the herbicide 2,4,5-T in national forests because it contained traces of dioxin, a suspected carcinogen.

Extremely low frequency (50–60 Hz) electromagnetic fields (ELF-EMFs) have been linked by some studies to leukemia and brain cancer in children and adults. The evidence for the connection is conflicting and highly controversial. ELF-EMFs are emitted by electricity moving through any electric circuit. Some researchers think that ELF-EMFs generated by electric blankets, cellular phones, and other household appliances, and by power lines increase the risk of cancer. Concern was first raised about ELF-EMFs and cancer in 1979. Critics of the EMF-cancer connection point out that the rapid growth in the use of electricity has not been paralleled by a great increase in cancer rates. What is needed, they say, is a test using laboratory cells that will show a consistent and reproducible response to ELF-EMFs, and an understanding of the mechanism through which ELF-EMFs affect cells.

Prevention of Cancer

(See also "Causes of Cancer," page 8; "Diet and Cancer," page 28; "Tobacco and Cancer," page 72.)

Cancer prevention can occur at three levels: primary, secondary, and tertiary.

Primary prevention means preventing or eliminating exposure to substances that cause cancer. The goal is to prevent the cancer process from starting. Not smoking, avoiding sunburn and ionizing radiation, avoiding infection by cancer viruses, and eliminating carcinogens in the workplace are examples of primary prevention.

Primary prevention can be accomplished only after the cause of a cancer is known. If the cause remains unknown, then secondary prevention— early detection and screening—is necessary. The goal is to catch cancer early to improve the odds of successful treatment.

Secondary prevention includes the Pap test for cervical cancer, breast self-exams and mammography for breast cancer, digital rectal exams for prostate cancer, and testicular self-exams for testicular cancer. Information on how to perform breast and testicular self-exams can be obtained from the American Cancer Society or the National Cancer Institute (call the Cancer Information Service at 1-800-4-CANCER).

Tertiary prevention refers to the treatment of cancer patients. The goals are to prevent premature death and maintain quality of life.

Proteins and Protein Synthesis

Proteins are compounds made up of one or more chains of amino acids. The importance of proteins to the cell cannot be overemphasized. For example, the chemical messengers that tell cells to grow and multiply—growth factors and many hormones—are proteins. Hormones and growth factors attach to receptor molecules—cellular off-and-on switches—and spark cell division. The receptors are proteins. The receptors trigger a cascade of chemical reactions within the cell that end in cell division. These and all chemical reactions in the cell are controlled by enzymes. Enzymes are proteins.

Proteins also make up the mechanism that causes muscles to contract, the antibodies and immunoglobulins in the immune system, and the microtubules and microfilaments that form the skeletal framework of the cell and of the connective tissues in the body.

The cell makes proteins (Fig. 6) by attaching smaller molecules—amino acids—end to end to form a chain. Most proteins are between 50 and 500 amino acids long, but they can also be shorter or longer. This chain is then folded into its final shape. Proteins can be helical, or form sheets

Figure 6 (opposite). Protein synthesis begins when a gene is turned on, or activated. During gene activation, the two strands of the DNA double helix open along the length of the gene. A strand of messenger RNA (mRNA) forms along the open edge of the DNA (top of diagram). This happens through complementary base pairing (see "DNA," page 31). The mRNA forms with the help of an enzyme, RNA polymerase, which is shaped like a sphere with a concavity. This first stage of protein synthesis is known as transcription.

The mRNA, which is a copy of the gene, is then edited. Segments of unneeded information—introns—are cut out of the mRNA strand, and the segments of needed genetic information—exons—are stitched together (center of diagram). The mature mRNA molecule then leaves the nucleus and enters the cytoplasm.

In the cytoplasm, ribosomes attach to the mRNA and assembly of the protein begins (bottom of diagram). Assembly occurs with the help of another form of RNA, transfer RNA (tRNA). tRNA transports individual amino acids to the ribosome–mRNA complex. There, the amino acids are added to the lengthening protein. Which amino acid is needed next is specified by the genetic code in the mRNA. In the genetic code, a series of three bases corresponds to one amino acid. This three-base sequence is known as a codon. This final phase of protein synthesis is known as translation.

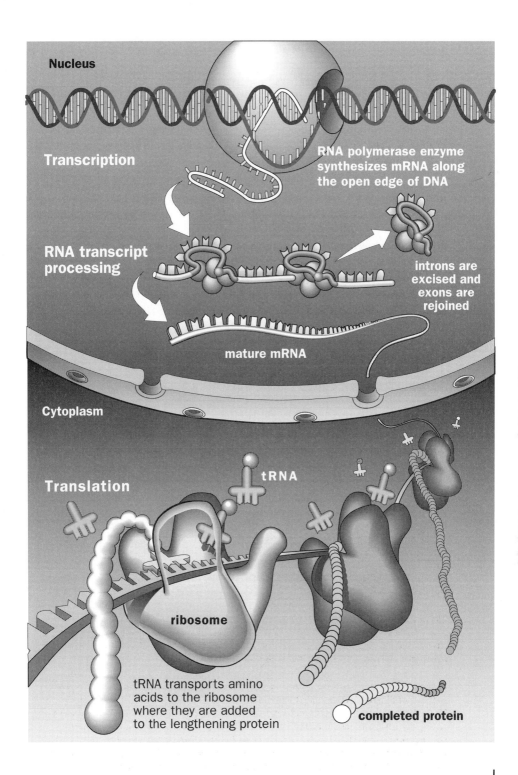

or globules, for example. At this point, a protein is usually active and ready for service. How does the cell know the number and sequence of amino acids that go into a particular protein? That is the information contained in genes. Through the sequence of bases in its DNA, a gene describes the structure of a protein (or one chain in a protein). That structure is imparted to the protein through the process of protein synthesis.

The flow of information that occurs during protein synthesis is the "central dogma" of biology. It can be summarized as follows:

DNA—>RNA—>protein

That is, the production of a protein begins with the information in DNA. That information is copied, or transcribed, in the form of RNA. The message contained in the RNA is then translated into a protein (Fig. 6). The only organisms on Earth that don't follow this path are the retroviruses, which carry their genetic information in the form of RNA instead of DNA. This adds one more step to the flow of information:

RNA—>DNA—>RNA—>protein

A change in the sequence of bases in DNA—a mutation—will alter the sequence of amino acids in a protein. That, in turn, will change the structure of the protein during protein synthesis. If the change occurs in a critical region of the protein, it can inactivate the molecule and perhaps cause the death of the cell. If the change occurs in a nonessential region of the protein, it may not affect the action of the molecule, resulting in a "silent mutation." In rare cases, a mutation will improve the action of a protein. This may give a survival advantage to those of the species carrying the mutation and lead to evolutionary progress.

But usually, genetic mutations are not advantageous to the organism. Mutations in DNA that cause defective proteins are thought to be at the heart of cancer. For example, scientists think that cancer is triggered in part when carcinogens damage tumor suppressor genes—genes that produce a regulatory protein that suppresses cell division (see "Tumor Suppressor Genes," page 78). The mutations lead to a defective protein, one that has lost the ability to regulate cell division. Mutations in another category of genes, genes that also play a critical role in the regulation of cell division, can lead to the over-production of proteins. These mutations convert normal genes into oncogenes (see "Oncogenes," page 57). This is thought to be another important step in the development of cancer.

Risk and Cancer

The dictionary defines risk as the *possibility* of loss, injury, or disease. Epidemiologists, however, think of risk in terms of the *probability* of loss, injury, or disease. A probability is a calculation that estimates what is likely to happen in the future based on what has happened in the past.

Epidemiologists monitor the incidence of disease and use those numbers to calculate the probable risk of the disease to the general population. They also try to identify groups of people whose risk is higher than average for the disease, and they try to identify factors that might be responsible for that higher risk. It is important to keep in mind that epidemiological studies only point to an association between some factor and a disease—such as the association between cigarette smoking and lung cancer. They provide no evidence of cause and effect. For example, epidemiological studies show that a diet high in fruits, vegetables, and grains is associated with a reduced risk of cancer, but those studies shed no light on how or why such a diet reduces cancer risk. Researchers learn about cause and effect through laboratory experiments on animals or isolated cells, or through clinical research.

The U.S. does not have a national tumor registry that keeps track of cancer incidence and mortality. Instead, estimates of cancer risk in the U.S. are calculated through the cooperation of epidemiologists at the National Cancer Institute (NCI) and the American Cancer Society (ACS). For the most part, epidemiologists at the NCI (a government agency that is part of the National Institutes of Health) gather raw numbers on cancer incidence and survival through the NCI's Surveillance, Epidemiology, and End Results (SEER) program. The SEER program collects information on cancer incidence from nine areas of the nation. These include the entire states of Hawaii, Connecticut, Iowa, New Mexico, and Utah, and the metropolitan areas of Atlanta, Detroit, San Francisco–Oakland, and Puget Sound. SEER data encompass about 10 percent of the U.S. population. Epidemiologists with the ACS (the world's largest private cancer advocacy organization) use these numbers to calculate cancer incidence and mortality. There is a time lag of several years, however. Estimates of cancer incidence and survival for 1993, for example, are based on SEER data collected during 1987–89. These estimates are published annually in the ACS booklet *Cancer Facts and Figures*. The ACS also uses mortality figures from the National Center for Health Statistics to estimate cancer deaths in the U.S.; it calculates international cancer mortality rates using numbers reported by the World Health Organization. The ACS also publishes statistics produced by the NCI and the National Centers for Disease Control and Prevention.

The risk of developing cancer and other diseases is described in several ways. The most common are lifetime risk and relative risk.

Lifetime risk is the probability that an individual will develop cancer sometime between birth and death. The calculation takes into account the rate of newly diagnosed cancer in different age groups. The age groups run in five-year intervals to age 85. The calculation also takes into consideration the rate at which people die from other causes.

For example, the lifetime risk of breast cancer in American women is now one in eight (i.e., one woman in eight can expect to develop breast cancer sometime in her life). This is a frightening number that represents a serious problem. But it is also a little misleading because the risks are really very different for different age groups, particularly for pre- and postmenopausal women, as shown in the table.

Change in Risk of Developing Breast Cancer Over a Woman's Lifetime	
By age 25	1 in 19,608
By age 30	1 in 2,525
By age 35	1 in 622
By age 40	1 in 217
By age 45	1 in 93
By age 50	1 in 50
By age 55	1 in 33
By age 60	1 in 24
By age 65	1 in 17
By age 70	1 in 14
By age 75	1 in 11
By age 80	1 in 10
By age 85	1 in 9
Lifetime	1 in 8

Source: National Cancer Institute

Relative risk: The risk of developing a cancer is usually described in terms of relative risk. Relative risk is calculated by dividing the incidence rate of disease in a group exposed to a suspected carcinogen or risk factor by the incidence of disease in a nonexposed group. The relative risk for average smokers developing lung cancer, for example, is 9.9. This means that smokers are about ten times more likely to develop lung cancer relative to nonsmokers. That's a high relative risk. A relative risk of 1.0 indicates a risk no greater than that of the comparison group used in the study. A relative risk of less than 1.0 (e.g., 0.85) indicates lower risk, or a protective effect. Many relative risks are in the range of 1.3 or 1.5, meaning that the exposed person has a 30 percent or 50 percent greater chance of developing the disease than an unexposed person.

Relative risk can be directly calculated only from cohort studies. These are studies that compare groups of people—exposed and nonexposed—who are followed through time to see who develops the disease (i.e., they are prospective studies). The comparison allows the researcher to determine the incidence rates in the two groups. The incidence rates are then used to calculate the relative risk.

Odds ratio is an approximation of relative risk. It is used to estimate relative risk in case control studies. In a case control study, a researcher selects people with a disease (the "cases"), matches them with people who don't have the disease (the "controls"), and then uses interviews, questionnaires, and medical histories to identify a risk factor that might be responsible for the disease. Because case control studies look back in time (i.e., they are retrospective), incidence rates and relative risk cannot be directly calculated as in cohort studies (described above). Instead, relative risk for case control studies must be indirectly estimated using an odds ratio. An odds ratio is the odds that a patient was exposed to the potential risk factor divided by the odds that a control was exposed to the factor. Odds ratios are interpreted in the same way as relative risks.

Tobacco and Cancer

Tobacco use is linked to one-third of all cancers in the U.S. Tobacco use is a major cause of cancers of the mouth, pharynx, larynx, lung, and esophagus, and contributes to the development of cancers of the pancreas, uterine cervix, kidney, and bladder. Its use is also a major cause of heart disease and is associated with emphysema, colds, chronic bronchitis, gastric ulcers, and stroke (i.e., cerebrovascular disease).

Tobacco smoke contains more than 4,000 chemical compounds, at least 43 of which are carcinogens or suspected carcinogens. The drug nicotine is responsible for tobacco addiction.

The American Cancer Society estimates that cigarette smoking is responsible for 90 percent of lung cancer deaths among men and 79 percent among women. Lung cancer rates among women have more than doubled in the last 20 years; in 1986, lung cancer surpassed breast cancer as the leading cause of cancer deaths in women. These increases parallel the increase in cigarette smoking by women after a 20-year use interval.

Secondhand smoke—tobacco smoke in the environment—is estimated to be responsible for 53,000 deaths in the U.S. annually. Most are due to heart disease; about 4,000 are due to lung cancer. Secondhand smoke can also aggravate asthma and impair blood circulation

Smokeless tobacco consists of snuff and chewing tobacco in the U.S. Carcinogens associated with snuff include tobacco-specific nitrosamines and radiation-emitting polonium. The maximum levels of nitrosamines permitted by the FDA in foods are 5 to 10 ppb; the levels found in smokeless tobacco products range from 100 to 1,000 ppb. The risk of cancer of the cheek and gum can be 50 times greater among long-term snuff users compared to non-users. Smokeless tobacco use can also lead to nicotine addiction and dependence.

See "Causes of Cancer," page 8.

Treatment of Cancer

After cancer is diagnosed, an oncologist puts together a strategy—a treatment plan—that attempts either to cure the disease or relieve its symptoms, depending on the type and stage of cancer. A treatment plan may also include supportive care for prevention of nausea and vomiting, pain management, nutritional maintenance, and psychological counseling.

Three main approaches are used to treat cancer: surgery, radiation, and chemotherapy. Depending on the disease, they can be used alone or in combination. Immunotherapy—use of the immune system to treat cancer—is being accepted as a fourth method of cancer treatment. See "Immunotherapy and Cancer Vaccines," page 54.

Surgery is the oldest form of cancer treatment. Some of the developments in surgery that have improved cancer survival and quality of life include the following:

* Voice preservation and restoration surgery for laryngeal cancer.
* Interdisciplinary surgery to remove cancer involving the base of the cranium.
* Conservative breast surgery (lumpectomy rather than mastectomy).
* Laser surgery for obstructing throat, bronchial, and esophageal cancers.
* Limb-sparing surgery, which reduces the need to amputate arms and legs for treatment of sarcomas of the extremities. The patient retains the limb and a significant amount of movement.

Radiation therapy is the use of ionizing radiation to treat cancer. Ionizing radiation can be delivered using photon beams or particle beams. Photon beams consist of X-rays and gamma rays (identical to X-rays, but coming from a radioactive rather than an electronic source). Particle beams consist of electrons, neutrons, or, rarely, protons. Radiation therapy is used at some point in the treatment of more than half of all cancer cases. The dosages used are about half a million times greater than those used in the average chest X-ray. Radiation therapy works by breaking chemical bonds in DNA or by producing free radicals in the cell that damage DNA. The art of radiation therapy relates to maximizing the damage to tumor cells while minimizing damage to surrounding healthy tissue. New technologies that help this balancing act include the following:

- Computed tomography (CT) and magnetic resonance imaging (MRI), which provide better imaging of tumors.
- Brachytherapy, the placement of tiny sources of radiation in or near the tumor site.
- Three-dimensional planning, the use of computers to combine CT scans to produce a three-dimensional image and a precise location of the tumor.
- Conformational therapy, which involves shaping the radiation field to conform to the contour of the tumor, thereby sparing healthy tissues.

Chemotherapy is the use of drugs to treat cancer that may have spread and therefore been missed by surgery or radiation therapy. For the types of drugs used, see "Chemotherapy for Cancer," page 19.

Tumor Markers, Serum

Serum tumor markers are substances in the blood that when found in high levels indicate the possible presence of a malignancy.

The substances used as serum tumor markers can be proteins (antigens), hormones, or enzymes. They are given off in very low levels by healthy cells but at much higher levels by cancer cells. For this reason, they provide only suggestive evidence that cancer is present. Whether cancer really is present must be confirmed by further testing. Tumor markers are most useful to detect recurrence of disease in patients who have already been treated. For example, a man with prostate cancer is likely to have elevated levels of prostatic specific antigen (PSA) in his blood. After treatment, the level of PSA should be much lower. If the level begins to rise in subsequent months or years, it is good evidence that the tumor has recurred.

Frequently Mentioned Serum Tumor Markers and the Cancers with Which They Are Associated

Tumor marker	Associated malignancy
Carcinoembryonic antigen (CEA)	Tumors of the colon, lung, breast, ovary
Human chorionic gonadotropin (HCG)	Trophoblastic and testicular tumors
Alpha-fetoprotein (AFP)	Testicular and liver cancers
Prostatic acid phosphatase (PAP)	Prostate cancer
Prostatic specific antigen (PSA)	Prostate cancer
CA-125	Epithelial ovarian cancer
CA 19-9	Cancer of the pancreas and colon

Tumor Staging and Grading

Tumor staging is the process of identifying the type and degree of a patient's cancer. Tumor staging must be done accurately. It helps a physician determine the seriousness of a patient's cancer and how it should be treated. Tumor staging allows clinicians in different hospitals to compare similar patients in their response to treatment. It also helps ensure that patients in the same stage of disease are compared during drug studies. A number of staging systems are in use, but one that is internationally accepted is the TNM system (TNM for Tumor, Node, Metastasis). The TNM system is a way of classifying the size of a tumor and the degree to which it has spread through the body. This information is then used to determine the stage of disease. The following is presented as a simplified idea of how the TNM system works (the exact definition of each level in the TNM system varies with the type of cancer):

"T" indicates the size, depth, and area of the primary tumor.
> TX: primary tumor cannot be assessed.
> T0: no evidence of a primary tumor.
> Tis: carcinoma in situ (the malignant cells are confined to the epithelial layer of the tissue).
> T1: localized tumor 2 centimeters (about three-quarters of an inch) or less in diameter and confined to the organ of origin.
> T2: localized tumor less than 5 centimeters (2 inches) in diameter that extends into adjacent tissue of the same organ.
> T3: advanced tumor greater than 5 centimeters (2 inches) in diameter with greater involvement of adjacent tissue of the same organ.
> T4: massive tumor that extends into nerves, blood vessels, bone, or some other organ.

"N" indicates whether the cancer has spread to regional lymph nodes. It records the number and mobility of affected nodes.
> NX: regional lymph nodes cannot be assessed.
> N0: no evidence of metastases to regional lymph nodes.
> N1, N2, N3: increasing involvement of regional lymph nodes.

"M" notes the presence or absence of distant metastases.

MX: distant metastases cannot be assessed.

M0: no evidence of metastasis.

M1: distant metastasis present.

Once the T, N, and M classifications are made, they are combined to determine the stage of the patient's cancer. In general, the higher the stage of disease, the lower the odds that treatment will be successful. The following is one example of how the TNM system might be used to stage cancer:

Stage I: T1 N0 M0

Stage II: T2 N1 M0

Stage III: T3 N0 M0
T1–3 N1 M0

Stage IV: T4 N0–1 M0
T0–4 N2–3 M0
T0–4 N0–4 M1

Tumor grading means categorizing a tumor according to the microscopic appearance of its cells and is another measure of the type and aggressiveness of the disease. It is done by a pathologist. Tumor grading is based on the degree of differentiation of the cancer cells, and on the cancer's growth rate. The growth rate is estimated based on the number of cancer cells undergoing division in a sample of tumor tissue.

Both criteria attempt to measure the degree to which the tumor cells differ from their normal counterparts. Cancer cells that are well differentiated resemble their normal cells, whereas cells that are poorly differentiated or undifferentiated bear little resemblance to normal cells in that tissue. Tumors composed mainly of undifferentiated cells tend to be more aggressive—faster growing—that those that are well differentiated.

Tumor Suppressor Genes

Tumor suppressor genes normally produce certain proteins that suppress cell division. When a tumor suppressor gene is lost or damaged, the control that it executed on cell growth is lost, thereby triggering cancer. (Note that tumor

Tumor Suppressor Genes Associated with Human Tumors	
Name	*Tumor involvement*
Retinoblastoma _____	Retinoblastoma
p53 _____	Numerous cancers
DCC _____	Colon
Wilms _____	Kidney
FCC _____	Hereditary colon cancer

suppressor genes lead to cancer through loss of action. This is in contrast to oncogenes, which lead to cancer through overaction.)

The discovery of tumor suppressor genes was as important to understanding cancer as was the discovery of oncogenes. The inactivation of tumor suppressor genes is now thought to be a necessary step in the development of human cancer.

The two best understood tumor suppressor genes are the retinoblastoma gene and the gene known as p53.

The study of retinoblastoma, a malignant tumor of the eye in young children, led to the discovery of tumor suppressor genes in 1990. Researchers found that both copies of the retinoblastoma (Rb) gene were often inactive in cancer cells from Rb tumors. Everyone is born with two copies of the Rb gene, one from the mother and one from the father. In most children, both copies are normal, healthy genes. Many children with familial Rb, however, are born with a copy that is defective. The tumor doesn't occur so long as the one good copy remains healthy. Often, though, a random mutation disables the healthy gene, and the tumor develops. Rb that arises in a family for the first time—non-familial Rb—is thought to result from random mutation of both copies of the Rb gene in a cell of the retina.

The p53 gene, which is mutated in about half of human tumors at multiple organ sites, is thought to be the most frequently mutated gene in human cancer. It has been found in a variety of tumors, including those of the colon, brain, lung, and breast, and in leukemias and osteosarcomas. The inheritance of a mutated copy of the p53 gene is thought responsible for the familial occurrence of some of these cancers through the same mechanism as familial Rb, described above.

Ultraviolet Light, Ozone, Tanning Beds, and Cancer

Ultraviolet (UV) light is a component of sunlight that is invisible to the human eye. It is also a very energetic form of light. It causes sunburn and can cause skin cancers (squamous cell carcinoma, basal cell carcinoma, and malignant melanoma). UV is separated according to wavelength into three classes: A, B, and C. The shorter the wavelength, the more energy is carried in the light.

Class	Wavelength (in nanometers)
A	320–400
B	280–320
C	280–100

Life on Earth is protected from harmful UV rays by the ozone layer. This is a region of concentrated ozone gas in the outer stratosphere some 130 miles above the Earth. The ozone layer blocks some UV-A radiation, 90 to 99 percent of UV-B, and nearly all UV-C, the most energetic of UV radiation.

UV-B causes sunburn and can cause chronic skin damage and cancer. Long exposure to UV-A will also damage the skin and cause cancer. UV-A is considered to be a promoter (see "Carcinogenesis," page 6) for skin cancer in mice.

A number of human-produced chemicals, especially certain chlorofluorocarbons (CFCs) used as refrigerants and to make Styrofoam, react with and destroy ozone. Many scientists believe that the release of CFCs into the atmosphere has caused a thinning of Earth's ozone layer, particularly over the southern hemisphere. In some cases, this thinning has been dramatic, leading many scientists to fear that the loss of ozone will cause skin cancer rates to rise. A 1986 estimate by the Environmental Protection Agency predicts that every 1 percent decrease in the ozone layer will cause a 2–5 percent rise in squamous cell carcinoma and a 1–3 percent rise in basal cell carcinoma. A Norwegian study estimated that a 10 percent depletion of the ozone layer would increase basal cell carcinoma cases by 16–18 percent, and malignant melanoma cases by 19 percent in men and 32 percent in women.

Tanning-bed lamps are another source of UV light. Their radiation is mostly UV-A, but as much as 3 percent can be UV-B. One estimate indicated that users of tanning booths can receive doses of UV-B comparable to an hour or more of noon sun and doses of UV-A that are much greater than normal. Furthermore, if UV-A proves to be a tumor promoter in humans, as it is in mice, people exposing themselves first to the high UV-A in a tanning booth, then to the mixed UV-A and UV-B in sunlight, may be putting themselves at high risk for skin cancer.

Viruses and Cancer

Virus infections are linked to 10 to 15 percent of cancers worldwide. About 80 percent of these are cancers of the cervix and liver.

Viruses usually do not induce cancer by themselves, nor do all people infected with the virus develop cancer. Rather, viruses are thought to be one factor that acts at an early stage in the process that leads to cancer, which develops only after exposure to one or more cofactors (Table 3). Viruses generally help cause malignancy either by introducing an oncogene into a cell or by inserting viral DNA into the genome of the host cell in ways that disrupt the regulation of cell division.

Epstein-Barr virus (EBV) is a member of the human herpesvirus family. It can be present in 50 to 100 percent of a population, even in affluent countries. The virus is found in nearly all Burkitt's lymphoma tumors from patients in central Africa, where the disease is most common. Outside of Africa, the virus is found in only 15 to 20 percent of the lymphomas in patients with Burkitt's lymphoma (the disease is rare in the U.S.). The role of EBV in nasopharyngeal carcinoma, B-cell lymphoma, and Hodgkin's disease is poorly understood.

Hepatitis B virus (HBV) causes hepatitis B and plays a major role in the development of a form of liver cancer known as hepatocellular carcinoma (HCC). Some 300 million people in underdeveloped countries are thought to carry the virus; three-fourths of these people are in Asia. Malignancy may not develop for 30 to 50 years after infection. In underdeveloped countries, transmission most often occurs from mother to child during birth, although the virus can also be passed by blood, saliva, and semen.

Human immune deficiency virus (HIV), the retrovirus that causes HIV disease, has not been isolated from tumor cells, but people with advanced HIV disease (i.e., acquired immune deficiency syndrome, or AIDS), often develop characteristic tumors. One of these, Kaposi's sarcoma, was an early diagnostic feature of the disease. Prior to HIV disease, this was a rare tumor most often seen in elderly men. Those with advanced HIV disease are also at high risk for lymphoma, and anal-genital warts, which often precede anal and genital cancers. Women with advanced HIV disease are at increased risk of cervical cancer. There also is

Table 3. Viruses associated with human tumors.

Name of Virus	Type of Cancer	Cofactors
Epstein-Barr virus (EBV)	Burkitt's lymphoma	Malaria
	Nasopharyngeal carcinoma	Nitrosamines
	B-cell lymphoma	Immunodeficiency
	Hodgkin's disease	Unknown
Hepatitis B virus (HBV)	Liver cancer	Aflatoxin, alcohol
Human immune deficiency virus (HIV)	Causes severe immune deficiency, which predisposes patients to Kaposi's sarcoma, lymphoma, and cervical cancer	EBV, HPV, herpes viruses
Human papilloma-virus (HPV)	Cervical	Smoking
	Skin (in some people with epidermodysplasia verruciformis, a rare hereditary condition)	Sunlight
Human T-cell lymphotropic virus Type 1 (HTLV-1)	Adult T-cell Leukemia/lymphoma (ATL)	Unknown
Human T-cell lymphotropic virus Type 2 (HTLV-2)	Hairy cell leukemia	Unknown
Kaposi's-sarcoma-associated herpesvirus (KSHV)	Kaposi's sarcoma	Unknown
	Body-cavity-based lymphoma	EBV and HIV

evidence that Kaposi sarcoma and lymphoma in HIV patients develop as a result of the immunodeficiency resulting from destruction of T-lymphocytes by HIV.

Human papillomaviruses (HPV) are a large group of viruses that infect animals from birds to humans. Some types of human papillomavirus cause cancer. They have been linked to anal and genital cancers, cancer of the cervix. Epidemiological studies show a pattern of infection that suggests venereal spread. Multiple sex partners and early onset of sexual activity are risk factors for cervical cancer.

Human T-cell lymphotropic virus Type 1 (HTLV-1) is a retrovirus found primarily in populations in southern Japan, Brazil, the Caribbean, and regions of central Africa. It is associated with adult T-cell leukemia and lymphoma (ATL). Antibodies to the virus are present in more than a million people in southern Japan, but only one out of 25 to 30 of those will develop ATL. The disease may not appear until 30 to 40 years after infection (which usually occurs at birth or through breast feeding). Because the viral DNA doesn't always end up near the appropriate genes in the host cell, not everyone infected with HTLV-1 develops leukemia or lymphoma.

Human T-cell lymphotropic virus Type 2 (HTLV-2) is a retrovirus linked with hairy cell leukemia. Its connection with the disease is weak because it has been identified in cells from only a few patients with the disease.

Kaposi's-sarcoma-associated herpesvirus (KSHP) is a possible new herpes virus associated with Kaposi's sarcoma both in patients with and in patients without HIV disease. Evidence for this virus emerged in December 1994, but isolation and identification of the virus had yet to be accomplished as of May 1995. Evidence of KSHP has also been found in body-cavity-based lymphomas, suggesting that this virus may play a role in causing this unusual subgroup of malignant lymphomas. Body-cavity-based lymphomas are effusions of lymphocytes that occur in the lung cavity, the cavity containing the heart, or the abdominal cavity of some patients with advanced HIV disease.

Glossary

Terms in small capital letters were selected for cross-referencing.

adduct
See DNA ADDUCT.

adeno-
Prefix meaning "gland."

adenocarcinoma
A malignancy arising from the epithelium of a glandular organ.

adjuvant
In immunology, a substance that is included in a vaccine to help stimulate the immune system to respond to the antigen in the vaccine. An adjuvant can be a TOXOID or, sometimes, a BIOLOGICAL RESPONSE MODIFIER.

adjuvant therapy
Treatment given following surgery to help prevent a cancer's recurrence or to destroy cancer cells that have metastasized. Either chemotherapy, radiation therapy, or both are often given as adjuvant therapy.

agonist
A drug or chemical that binds to a cell receptor for a hormone, neurotransmitter, or growth factor and imitates the action of that substance.

alopecia
Hair loss.

American Cancer Society
The oldest private cancer advocacy organization in the world. It was organized by a group of citizens in 1913 as the American Society for the Control of Cancer. Compare with NATIONAL CANCER INSTITUTE.

amino acids
The building blocks of protein. There are 20 amino acids.

analog/analogue

A chemical or drug that is similar in structure to another; e.g., "The drug camptothechin has several analogs, one of which is topotecan."

androgen

A male sex hormone such as testosterone or androsterone.

angiogenesis

The formation of new blood vessels.

angiogram

X-ray of arteries or veins to look for blockages or abnormal placement of blood vessels. Used to help locate tumors.

antagonist

A drug or chemical that binds to a cell receptor for a hormone, neurotransmitter, or growth factor and blocks the action of that substance.

antibiotic

A natural or synthetic substance that kills microorganisms.

antibody

A protein produced by the immune system to bind to a specific ANTIGEN. Antibodies are receptor proteins found on or released by B CELLS.

antibody-mediated immune response (humoral immune response)

The antibody-mediated immune response produces antibodies in response to the presence of an ANTIGEN in the blood, mucous membranes, or extra-cellular fluids. It is effective against targets located outside cells. Compare with CELL-MEDIATED IMMUNE RESPONSE.

antigen

A substance, usually a protein, that stimulates formation of an ANTIBODY. Antibodies will then bind specifically to the antigen. This antigen-antibody complex serves as the basis for immunity. Examples of antigens include viruses, certain toxins, and components of bacteria and foreign cells. Antigens found on the surfaces of cells (cell-surface antigens) are important in the recognition of one cell by another.

antioxidant

A compound in some fruits and vegetables that is thought to reduce the damage caused by FREE RADICALS.

antisense strand
The strand of DNA in which the base pairs do not encode genetic information. If a length of DNA is unzipped down the middle, two strands result. One strand—the sense strand—carries genetic information. The other strand does not carry genetic information, and it is called the antisense strand.

antisense therapy
This is a strategy for blocking the action of one particular gene. The sequence of bases in the MESSENGER RNA (mRNA) for the gene, or the sequence of bases in the gene itself, must be known. A short piece of single-strand DNA is made in the laboratory. The length of DNA—known as an antisense OLIGONUCLEOTIDE—is complementary to the mRNA, which is also a single strand. The antisense oligonucleotide then binds to the mRNA through COMPLEMENTARY BASE PAIRING. The mRNA, which is now double-stranded, cannot bind with RIBOSOMES as it normally would and PROTEIN SYNTHESIS is blocked. The technique may one day provide a new treatment for cancer and other diseases.

apoptosis
Genetically programmed cell death. Apoptosis is a natural mechanism used by the body to eliminate cells that are no longer needed. It is also triggered by chemical carcinogens, certain anticancer drugs, and therapeutic doses of radiation, X-rays, and ultraviolet light. The blocking of apoptosis by certain mutations is now thought to play a role in triggering some cancers.

artery
Vessel that carries blood away from the heart (see VEIN).

-ase
A suffix that indicates an enzyme; e.g., "A lipase is an enzyme that breaks down lipids."

asymptomatic
Without symptoms.

atypical
Unusual; not conforming to the usual type.

autosomes
Chromosomes other than the X and Y sex chromosomes.

axilla
The armpit.

basal cell carcinoma
A type of skin cancer that rarely metastasizes but is highly invasive and destructive, penetrating both dermis and bone. It is highly curable if caught early.

base pairing
See COMPLEMENTARY BASE PAIRING.

basic research
Research that adds to the basic understanding of how nature works. A basic research study is done without regard to whether the results will have a specific application or immediate payoff. Rather, it is done to answer an interesting question. Basic research is the primary source of new scientific knowledge. In medicine, basic research is done in the laboratory using such things as flasks and test tubes, cultured cells, or animals. Compare with CLINICAL RESEARCH.

B cells
Lymphocytes that mature in the bone marrow. B cells produce antibodies, which recognize specific antigens. They form the branch of the immune system responsible for the ANTIBODY-MEDIATED IMMUNE RESPONSE, as opposed to the CELL-MEDIATED IMMUNE RESPONSE.

benign tumor
A tumor that is not cancerous. That is, it does not invade other tissues or metastasize. Benign tumors are rarely a threat to life, usually can be surgically removed, and usually do not recur.

bind
In molecular biology, one molecule clinging to another through chemical forces. Used as an adjective (e.g., "DNA-binding protein") or as a verb (e.g., "An antibody binds with its antigen").

binding protein/DNA-binding protein
Same as a REGULATORY PROTEIN.

biological response modifier
Broad term for natural and synthetic substances that influence the response of lymphocytes and other white cells to infection and tumors. Examples include cytokines, lymphokines, and growth factors such as granulocyte colony stimulating factor (G-CSF).

biopsy
Removal of a sample of tissue for microscopic examination to see if cancer cells are present.

bone marrow

The soft tissue that occupies the cavities inside bone. **Yellow marrow** fills the cavities of long bones. It consists of fat cells and connective tissue and does not participate in the formation of blood cells. **Red marrow** occupies the spongy cavities of the pelvis, ribs, sternum, vertebrae, skull, collarbones, and shoulder blades. Red marrow is where hemoglobin and red and white blood cells are produced.

bone marrow transplant (BMT)

A treatment for leukemia, lymphoma, multiple myeloma, aplastic anemia, ovarian, testicular, and possibly breast cancer. It involves removal and implantation of marrow or precursor cells from the bloodstream. The objective of the procedure is to restore the blood-forming cells destroyed by high-dose chemotherapy or radiation treatment for cancer. These cells are necessary for life. In an **allogenic** transplant, one person donates marrow to another; in an **autologous** transplant, the patient's own marrow is removed, sometimes treated to kill any cancer cells present, and returned to the patient following high-dose chemotherapy or radiation treatment.

brachytherapy

Radiation treatment in which tiny rods of a radioactive element are surgically placed in or near a tumor, giving the tumor a high dose of radiation. Brachytherapy literally means "treatment over a short distance."

C

cadherins

A class of cell receptor molecules that plays an important role in cell adhesion and sorting. A decrease in the functioning of cadherins is associated with the ability of tumor cells to invade other tissues.

cancer

Used to describe more than 100 different malignant tumors. It is characterized by uncontrolled cell growth and the ability of tumor cells to invade or spread (metastasize) to other tissues.

cancer cells

The cells present in malignant tumors. Characteristics that distinguish them from normal cells include irregular shape, changes in structure of NUCLEUS and CYTOPLASM, abnormal size of nucleus, abnormal number of chromosomes, increased number of cells undergoing cell division, and the ability to invade other tissues. Cells in culture that are cancerous feature additional characteristics that separate them from normal cells. These include not attaching to the bottom of the culture flask and growing in clusters several cell layers thick (healthy cells grow in a single layer).

cancer cluster
Occurrence of an unusually high number of cases of one type of cancer within a small geographic area.

cancer in situ/carcinoma in situ
Refers to an early stage of some cancers before the cancer has invaded other tissues. It is highly curable.

carcinogen
A substance or agent that increases the risk of cancer. Carcinogens can be chemicals, ionizing radiation, or viruses. (In 1990, rising cancer rates among black Americans prompted NCI head Samuel Broder to note that "poverty is a carcinogen.")

carcinoma
Cancer that arises from epithelial tissue—tissue that covers or lines organs of the body such as the lungs, liver, breast, and colon. Skin is also an epithelial tissue.

carcinoma in situ
See CANCER IN SITU.

case control study
Epidemiological study in which individuals with a particular disease—the cases—are compared with a group of closely matched individuals—the controls—who don't have the disease. It is a type of retrospective study. Researchers use interviews or questionnaires to help participants recall factors that might identify the cause of the disease or the risk factors associated with it. Compare with COHORT STUDY.

CD
Abbreviation for cluster of differentiation. It refers to an international system of nomenclature for lymphocytes and other white blood cells. The system is based on the use of monoclonal antibodies that react with receptors and other molecules on the surface of the cells. For example, if a lymphocyte reacts with the OKT4 antibody, it is said to be CD 4 positive (CD 4+). The CD classification helps identify a white cell's function and degree of maturity.

cDNA (DNA probe)
The "c" stands for complementary. cDNA, also known as a DNA probe, is a short single strand of DNA assembled in the laboratory that contains radioactive atoms. It is a DNA copy of a particular MESSENGER RNA (mRNA) isolated from cells. Since mRNA is a template of a gene (minus the INTRON segments), cDNA can be used to detect the presence of that particular mRNA produced by a cell. This, in turn, indicates the activity of the gene. cDNA is also used to locate the position of the gene on the chromosome.

cell
The fundamental building block of the body. Cells have two main regions, the NUCLEUS and the CYTOPLASM. Cells and their products make up all the tissues of the body. There are more than 200 different types of cells in the human body.

cell-mediated immune response
An immune response in which T lymphocytes destroy cells of the body infected with viruses, bacteria, and some fungi. The cell-mediated immune response locates and destroys pathogens that have made their way into body cells (which places them beyond reach of the ANTIBODY-MEDIATED IMMUNE RESPONSE). Cell-mediated immunity is also responsible for rejection of transplanted tissues and organs and for autoimmune diseases.

cell-surface receptors
Protein molecules on the cell surface that bind with such things as hormones, drugs, neurotransmitters, and growth factors. Contact between a molecule and a receptor triggers a change in the activity or behavior of the cell. Cells can have 500 to 100,000 receptors per cell; they can be spread diffusely over the surface or be clustered in a specific region of the membrane.

cervix
The neck-like region of an organ; e.g., the opening of the uterus or urinary bladder.

chemoprevention
Taking a drug or nutrient to prevent cancer before it occurs. A drug trial began in 1992 testing the use of the chemotherapy drug tamoxifen to prevent breast cancer in high-risk women.

chemotherapy
The use of drugs to treat cancer.

CIN
Cervical intraepithelial neoplasia. An early and pre-malignant stage of cervical cancer.

cis- and cis-acting
A prefix meaning on the same side. In genetics: refers to the location of two or more genes on the same chromosome. In molecular biology: cis-acting refers to a DNA BINDING SITE that acts only on the gene or genes adjacent to the site.

clinical research
Research, such as drug trials, that uses people. The goal is to prevent or treat disease. Compare with BASIC RESEARCH.

clone
A group of cells descended from a single cell. All the cells in the group are genetically identical.

co-carcinogen
A chemical or environmental agent that aggravates the action of a carcinogen.

codon
A group of three bases in messenger RNA that code for an amino acid; e.g., the codon UUU (three uracil bases in a row) is the genetic code for the amino acid phenylalanine, while the codon GCA (guanine, cytosine, adenine) codes for the amino acid alanine. Messenger RNA is a string of bases that represents a copy of the information in a gene. During protein synthesis, the cell "reads" this string of bases codon by codon (i.e., three bases at a time) to determine which amino acids should be added to the growing chain.

cohort study
An epidemiological study that compares a group of people (a cohort) that are known to have a disease to a group without the disease. It is a prospective study: researchers follow the participants forward in time to watch how the disease develops. Cohort studies also help identify risk factors for disease.

colon
The large intestine, which extends from the end of the small intestine to the rectum.

colonoscopy
Visual examination of the upper rectum by colonoscope.

colostomy
An opening from some area of the colon to the outside of the body. Permanent colostomies are seldom needed in colon cancer patients, and are used in only about 15 percent of patients with rectal cancer that is detected early.

combination chemotherapy
Use of two or more drugs to treat cancer.

combined modality therapy
Using more than one means to treat disease; for example, surgery plus radiation therapy for treatment of cancer.

complementary base pairing
In DNA, the matching of the base adenine with the base thymine, and the matching of the base cytosine with the base guanine. In RNA, the base uracil replaces thymine and pairs with adenine.

Comprehensive Cancer Centers, NCI-designated
Major hospitals, usually with medical schools, selected by the National Cancer Institute to serve as foci for cancer research, treatment, and outreach and prevention programs. They seek answers to high-priority questions and serve as sites for testing of new drugs.

computed tomography (CT) scan
Uses X-rays and a computer to produce cross-sectional images of the body. Also called computerized tomography.

cyst
A closed sac or pouch that contains fluid, semifluid, or a solid. It is usually an abnormal structure.

cytochrome P450 enzymes
A group of ENZYMES found in liver cells and others that detoxifies chemicals by metabolizing them. In the course of detoxifying chemical carcinogens, P450 enzymes produce substances that can damage DNA and lead to cancer.

cytokines
Hormone-like substances given off by lymphocytes and monocytes that help regulate cells that participate in the immune response. Lymphokines are cytokines given off by lymphocytes; monokines are cytokines given off by monocytes.

cytoplasm
The region of the cell outside the NUCLEUS. It contains most of the cell's organelles, including mitochondria, which produce energy; lysosomes, which contain enzymes; RIBOSOMES, which play a role in protein synthesis; and microtubules and microfilaments that form the skeleton of the cell.

D

dedifferentiation
The process whereby some cells, in the process of becoming cancerous, become less specialized and take on features and behavior—such as increased rate of cell division—of immature cells. See also DIFFERENTIATION.

Delaney Clause
Part of a food safety law passed in 1958 designed to keep carcinogens out of food.

differentiation
The process whereby immature cells become specialized. Tumors composed of differentiated cells are usually less aggressive than tumors composed of undifferentiated cells. See also DEDIFFERENTIATION.

digital rectal exam
Procedure in which a physician inserts a gloved finger into the rectum to feel the prostate gland for cancer.

DNA
Deoxyribonucleic acid. The molecule that encodes genetic information, and one of two nucleic acids (the other being RNA, or ribonucleic acid). DNA usually occurs as a double-stranded helix. Each chromosome is one molecule of DNA.

DNA adduct
A small molecule that can play a fundamental role in causing cancer. DNA adducts cling to DNA and must be removed by the cell before DNA can replicate. This can result in damage to the DNA, and therefore to a gene, and cancer can result. DNA adducts are usually produced by cells during the METABOLISM of certain chemicals known as pre-carcinogens. Several polyaromatic hydrocarbons are classic examples of pre-carcinogens that produce DNA adducts as products of metabolism.

DNA binding site
Location on a gene where a regulatory protein attaches.

DNA probe
See cDNA.

down-regulation
A decrease in the activity of a gene.

---

electron therapy
Radiation treatment using a beam of electrons. Most useful for treatment of superficial tumors.

ELF-EMFs
Extremely low frequency electromagnetic fields. ELF-EMFs are emitted by alternating electrical currents (A.C.) of 50–60 hertz as it flows through a circuit. Some research suggests that exposure to ELF-EMFs from power lines and household appliances such as electric blankets can lead to certain cancers. The conclusion that ELF-EMFs are associated with disease is highly controversial, however.

endocrine glands
Ductless glands that produce HORMONES and secrete them directly into the bloodstream.

endometrium
The mucous membrane that lines the uterus.

endoscopy
Examination of body organs or cavities using an endoscope, a tube-like device with a light and an optical system.

environment
When used in the context of cancer (e.g., "Many factors in the environment can lead to cancer."), environment refers to anything that humans interact with. This includes substances that are eaten, drunk, inhaled, smoked, and encountered in the work place. It also applies to taking drugs, exposure to radiation, and sexual behavior.

enzyme
A protein that greatly speeds up a chemical reaction. Enzymes are very specific in the reactions that they influence.

epidemiology
The study of incidence and distribution of disease in populations, and the relation between lifestyle, the environment, and disease.

epigenetic carcinogen
A chemical carcinogen that causes cancer without directly affecting DNA. Their mechanism of action is poorly understood. Examples include asbes-

tos; the synthetic estrogen, diethylstilbestrol; and carbon tetrachloride. One of two groups of chemical carcinogens, the other being GENOTOXIC CARCINOGENS.

epithelium/epithelial cells
The name given to issues that cover or line organs of the body. Examples include the skin, the linings of the lung and gastrointestinal tract, and the ducts of the breast and liver. Cells making up these tissues are epithelial cells.

estrogen
Hormone produced by the ovaries. It is essential for menstruation, reproduction, and development of female secondary sex characteristics such as breast enlargement. Estrogen inhibits certain cancers and promotes others.

etiology
Study of the cause of disease.

eukaryotic
Describes a cell or organism in which the chromosomes are gathered into a nucleus that is bound by a membrane. All higher organisms, from protozoa and yeast to mammals and trees, are composed of eukaryotic cells. See PROKARYOTIC.

exons
Segments of a gene containing the actual genetic information that describes the structure of a protein. See INTRONS.

external beam radiation
Radiation therapy that uses a machine outside the body to aim high-energy radiation at cancer cells.

F

familial
Relating to families; occurring in a family more often than would be expected by chance alone, as in "a familial disease."

fiber
Food components that are not broken down by the digestive system. Includes plant cell walls (cellulose), plant gums, algal polysaccharides, pectin, and methyl cellulose, which is man-made.

fibroadenoma
Benign tumors of the breast common in young women.

fibroblast
Cell or corpuscle that produces connective tissue.

first-degree relatives
Those that share half your genes (mother, father, sister, brother, children).

free radicals
Highly reactive molecules that are produced in cells by ultraviolet light, IONIZING RADIATION, and by the metabolism of chemical carcinogens. Free radicals have one or more unpaired electrons that react with and damage DNA and the cell membrane in ways that can lead to cancer.

frozen tissue section
Tissue that has been frozen, thinly sliced, and stained for viewing under the microscope. This is a rapid means of preparing tissues obtained by BIOPSY or during MOHS' SURGERY to see if malignant cells are present.

G

gamma rays
Same as X-rays, but gamma rays emanate from a radioactive source.

gene
A length of DNA that carries the genetic information necessary for production of a PROTEIN. The gene is also the basic unit of heredity. Genes are located on chromosomes.

gene expression
Refers to the production of messenger RNA or PROTEIN by an active gene.

gene product
The product of a gene is an RNA, a PROTEIN, or a PEPTIDE.

genetic code
The correspondence between the sequence of bases, first in DNA and then in RNA, and the specific sequence of amino acids in a protein. It is the basic language of protein synthesis, in which three bases of RNA specify one of the 20 amino acids. Such a group of base triplets is known as a CODON.

genome
All the genes possessed by an organism.

genotoxic carcinogen
A chemical carcinogen that causes cancer by damaging DNA. One of two groups of chemical carcinogens, the other being EPIGENETIC CARCINOGENS.

germ cells

The reproductive cells in the body; that is, eggs and sperm or their precursor cells. Mature eggs and sperm each carry 23 chromosomes, or one set from each parent. Fertilization of the egg by the sperm brings the two sets together to give the embryo the normal number of chromosomes, which is 46 in humans. Genetic mutations in germ cells can be transmitted to a person's offspring. A mutation in a SOMATIC CELL, on the other hand, may lead to cancer in the individual, but it will not be passed along to offspring.

granulocyte

A granulocyte is a white blood cell that contains granules in the cytoplasm when stained and viewed through a microscope. A granulocyte can be neutrophil, an eosinophil, or a basophil.

gray

A measurement of absorbed radiation dose. 1 gray = 100 RADS.

growth factor

A substance that influences growth by regulating the rate at which cells divide.

H

hematopoiesis

Production and development of blood cells.

hemoccult blood test

See STOOL BLOOD TEST.

hereditary

Used to describe genetic characteristics transferred from parent to offspring.

heterozygosity, loss of

In the context of tumor suppressor genes, refers to the condition in which both healthy copies of a tumor suppressor gene are lost. This inactivates the tumor suppressor gene and leaves the person more susceptible to cancer.

high risk

When the odds of developing cancer are greater than for the general population.

Hodgkin's disease
Cancer of the lymphatic system, producing enlargement of lymph nodes, spleen, and liver; and leading to progressive anemia.

hormone
A substance produced by an organ or gland that is carried by the blood and produces a specific effect on other organs or glands. Most hormones fall into two main groups: steroid and nonsteroid. **Steroid hormones** (e.g., cortisone, estrogen, testosterone) are produced from cholesterol, are soluble in fats, and easily cross the cell membrane. **Nonsteroid hormones** (e.g., epinephrine, insulin) are produced from amino acids, are soluble in water, and do not cross the cell membrane.

hormone therapy
The use of estrogen and progesterone to treat the symptoms of menopause in postmenopausal women.

hydrophobic/hydrophilic
Literally, water hating and water loving. Hydrophobic substances are usually soluble in fats; hydrophilic substances are soluble in water. Used in reference to compounds, molecules, and parts of molecules (e.g., oil is hydrophobic; sugar is hydrophilic).

hyperthermia
Literally, high temperature. Unusually high fever; in cancer, a radiation treatment that kills cancer cells by raising the temperature of the tumor.

hypoxia
Oxygen deficiency.

---

immunology
Study of the immune system and immunity to disease.

immunosurveillance
Recognition and destruction of abnormal cells by the immune system.

immunotherapy
Treatment of disease by stimulating or enhancing the immune system.

implant
See RADIOACTIVE IMPLANT.

incidence
The rate of new cases of a disease in a population over a specific period of time. See PREVALENCE.

induction chemotherapy
Use of drugs as the primary treatment of advanced cancer.

initiation
The first of two events that are thought to occur in cells during chemical carcinogenesis. Initiation happens when a chemical carcinogen damages DNA in a cell. The second event is promotion, which occurs when initiated cells are exposed to substances known as PROMOTERS.

in situ
Literally, in place.

in situ hybridization
Technique using radiolabeled RNA or DNA probes to locate specific DNA base sequences in chromosomes and RNA base sequences in cells.

interferon
A family of cytokines that have antiviral, antitumor, and immuno-modulating activity. There are three types of interferons: alpha interferon, produced by LEUKOCYTES; beta interferon, produced by FIBROBLASTS; and gamma interferon, produced by LYMPHOCYTES. Interferons are also synthetically produced. Alpha and beta are also known as type-1 interferon; gamma is known as type-2 interferon.

interleukin
A hormone—a CYTOKINE—released by lymphocytes. At least 12 kinds have been found. IL-2 has made it possible to culture T lymphocytes outside the body.

intraoperative radiation therapy
The use of radiation therapy during surgery.

introns
Segments of DNA that reside between EXONS in a gene. Introns can themselves have functions. Some, for example, are involved in gene control. Introns are cut out of a molecule of MESSENGER RNA before it leaves the nucleus during protein synthesis.

involuntary smoking
Exposure to tobacco smoke in the environment. Environmental tobacco smoke—or secondhand smoke—causes an estimated 53,000 deaths annually in the U.S., about two-thirds of them due to heart disease and about 4,000 from lung cancer. Can also aggravate asthma and impair blood circulation.

ion

An atom that bears an electrical charge. An ion results when a neutral atom gains or loses one or more electrons.

ionizing radiation

Radiation such as X-rays or gamma rays that can strip electrons from atoms or molecules. Ionizing radiation can damage DNA and other components of the cell and lead to cell death or cancer. Ionizing radiation is also used in radiation therapy to destroy cancer cells.

isotopes

Atoms of an element that have the same number of protons but a different number of neutrons (i.e., atoms that have the same atomic number but a different atomic weight). Carbon, for example, has three isotopes: carbon-12, carbon-13, and carbon-14. All carbon atoms have six protons, but isotopes of carbon can have 12, 13, or 14 neutrons. Some isotopes are radioactive; these are known as radioisotopes.

K

Karnovsky scale

A 100-point scale or index used to estimate a patient's physical state and performance. Karnovsky scores are often used to help determine a patient's prognosis. Scores range from 100 for perfectly well to 0 for dead.

kb and kbp

Kilobases and kilobase pairs. These are measures of length on a strand of DNA or within a gene. Refers to the number of bases in thousands; e.g., "the size of the acid fibroblast growth factor gene is more than 100 kb (that is, more than a 100,000 bases)."

L

laryngectomy

Surgical removal of the larynx, which contains the vocal cords.

leucine zipper

A molecular structure that holds two proteins together to form a single unit. Found on some regulatory proteins. Molecules of leucine (an amino acid) attract one another. Some proteins have a row or column of leucine molecules that point outward. When two such proteins come near one another, the two rows of leucine molecules join like the teeth in a zipper. The two proteins are then joined as a pair, forming a unit known as a dimer. The leucine zipper holds the dimer together in a specific way, allowing it to attach to a precise location on a gene (i.e., on DNA). This mechanism turns some genes on or off.

leukemia

Leukemia is a malignancy of blood-forming tissues. Leukemias are usually described as acute or chronic. These can be divided into four major
types. Acute leukemia can be lymphoblastic (ALL) or nonlymphoblastic
(ANLL). Chronic leukemia can be lymphocytic (CLL) or myelocytic
(CML). The names of these four types of leukemia refer to the type of
cell that becomes malignant. ALL arises in LYMPHOCYTE precursor cells;
ANLL develops in GRANULOCYTE precursor cells. CLL arises in lymphocytes, usually in B CELLS but sometimes in T CELLS; CML is characterized
by the presence of granulocytic cells in all stages of maturity. Acute leukemias usually arise in undifferentiated cells. Such cells have a high rate of
cell division, so the disease progresses rapidly; chronic leukemias occur in
more mature cells that have a slower rate of cell division, so these diseases
progress more slowly.

leukocytes

White blood cells or corpuscles. They include granulocytes (neutrophils,
basophils, and eosinophils), lymphocytes, and monocytes.

leukoplakia

Precancerous white patches on the mucous membrane of the cheek or
tongue. The patches do not necessarily become cancerous.

ligand

General term for a molecule that binds to another molecule. Often used
in reference to molecules that bind to cell receptors. These include hormones, drugs, neurotransmitters, and growth factors.

ligase chain reaction (LCR)

A laboratory technique that duplicates only those stretches of DNA that
have the exact genetic sequences being sought. Introduced in 1991, LCR
greatly enhances the ability to quickly identify the presence of specific genetic mutations.

linear accelerator

A machine that boosts charged particles such as electrons or protons to
enormous speeds to produce beams of gamma rays, X-rays, or neutrons.
Hospitals use linear accelerators in cancer therapy to generate gamma
rays and electron beams.

linkage map, genetic

A genetic linkage map specifies the relative position of genes or genetic
markers on chromosomes according to how often they are inherited together. If two genes or markers are almost always inherited together, they
are said to be closely linked.

localized cancer
Cancer that has not spread beyond the tissue in which it originated.

longitudinal study
Same as a PROSPECTIVE STUDY.

lumpectomy
Removal of a breast tumor only and leaving the rest of the breast tissue intact. The current standard treatment for breast tumors less than about one inch in diameter.

lymph
Clear, colorless fluid of the lymphatic system. Similar to blood, but without red cells. Formed in tissue spaces all over the body.

lymph glands/lymph nodes
Rounded bodies that vary in size from a pinhead to an olive and that are found at intervals along lymphatic vessels. They filter lymph and add lymphocytes to the system. They are clustered in the neck, the armpits, the crotch, and along the great blood vessels of the abdomen.

lymphocyte/lymphoblast
A type of white blood cell that is involved in the immune response to viruses and tumors. Lymphoblasts give rise to lymphocytes.

lymphokine
CYTOKINE given off by lymphocytes.

lymphokine-activated killer (LAK) cells
T CELLS that have been exposed to interleukin 2 and have the ability to destroy some tumor cells. See INTERLEUKIN.

lymphatic system
A separate system of vessels that assists the veins in returning fluids from the tissues. The lymph system empties into large veins at the base of the neck.

lymphoma
Malignancy or cancer of tissues of the lymphatic system. Major kinds include Hodgkin's disease and non-Hodgkin's lymphoma. Rarer forms include Burkitt's lymphoma.

macronutrient
A food necessary in relatively large quantities for the growth and well-being of an organism.

magnetic resonance imaging (MRI)
A technology that uses a strong magnetic field to generate diagnostic images of soft tissues such as the brain, heart, and major blood vessels. It does not involve exposure to radiation.

malignant tumor
A tumor that invades other tissues; a cancerous tumor.

mammogram
An X-ray of the breast.

melanoma, malignant
The most serious of skin cancers. It is a malignancy of pigment cells in the skin, eye, and mucous membranes. Depending on its location, malignant melanoma can spread quickly and cause death within months of diagnosis, while other forms of skin cancer—basal cell and squamous cell carcinomas—have extremely high five-year survival rates.

messenger RNA (mRNA)
A single strand of RNA that copies the "message" contained in a gene and carries it from the nucleus to the cytoplasm. There, the message is translated into a protein (see TRANSLATION).

meta-analysis
A statistical method that combines the results of already completed studies of a drug or treatment that have been done by different people. Meta-analysis results in a larger experimental population to assess the effects of a new drug or treatment. Meta-analysis must be carefully designed to best use available data and to avoid the possibility of biased results.

metabolic activation
The process in which cells convert a chemical pre-carcinogen into a carcinogen. Some drugs require metabolic activation in order to work.

metabolism
The chemical changes that take place in an organism or cell. These changes produce the energy and materials needed by cells to live and grow. They include anabolism (the building of components needed by the cell) and catabolism (the breaking down of substances, such as sugar, usually with the release of heat and usable energy).

metabolite
Any of the chemical products of metabolism.

metastasis
Spread of cancer cells from the primary tumor to another part of the body, usually via the bloodstream or lymph system. The ability of cancer cells to metastasize makes them malignant and sets them apart from benign tumors.

micrometastases
Microscopic clusters of tumor cells that have spread from the primary tumor to a lymph node or other area of the body. Micrometastases develop and grow to become metastatic tumors.

micronutrient
A nutrient required in small amounts.

mitosis
The process of cell division. By the time it occurs, DNA has replicated, producing two sets of chromosomes. Mitosis begins when DNA condenses and the chromosomes become shortened and thickened, and the nuclear membrane breaks down. The chromosomes then line up at the center of the cell. Next, the chromosomes are separated and dragged to opposite ends of the cell. Mitosis ends when the thickened chromosomes uncoil, and two nuclei form. The cytoplasm then divides, producing two daughter cells, each with a complete set of chromosomes. Many chemotherapeutic drugs target mitotic cells. These include fast-growing tumor cells, cells in hair follicles, and those lining the intestine. The drugs interfere with the machinery of mitosis. Mitotic cells are also more sensitive to radiation treatment.

Mohs' surgery
Surgery done to remove skin cancers on areas of the body such as the nose, ears, and genitals where little excess skin is available for excision. Especially useful for basal cell carcinoma.

molecular epidemiology
Looks for consistent patterns of DNA damage following exposure to specific carcinogens. These patterns of DNA damage are known as biomarkers or molecular fingerprints.

molecule
The smallest entity to which a substance may be reduced without loss of the substance's chemical characteristics; e.g., H_2O—two atoms of hydrogen attached to one atom of oxygen—is one molecule of water.

monoclonal antibody (MAb)

A highly specific antibody produced in the laboratory for detection of particular proteins or parts of proteins. Fluorescent or radioactive labels can be attached to MAbs to locate such things as the presence of the protein in a blood sample, the occurrence of receptor molecules on the surface of a cell, or the presence of certain cancers in tissues.

monokine

CYTOKINE given off by monocytes, a type of white blood cell.

morbidity rate

The number of people with a specific disease per unit of population. The units are usually 10,000 or 100,000 people.

mortality rate

The death rate. The number of people who have died from a specific cause per unit of population.

murine

Having to do with rodents, especially rats and mice.

mutagen

A substance that causes genetic mutations. Mutagens include chemicals, medicines, ionizing radiation, and ultraviolet light.

mutation

A change in a gene. Mutations that occur in eggs and sperm can be passed along to offspring; mutations that occur in other cells of the body (i.e., somatic cells) sometimes lead to cancer.

N

National Cancer Institute (NCI)

The U.S. government's largest cancer research facility. It is also the largest of the institutes in the National Institutes of Health. It has researchers on the NCI campus in Bethesda, Maryland, and funds cancer research centers at major universities in the U.S. and other countries.

natural killer (NK) cells

Lymphocyte-like cells that destroy virus-infected cells and some tumor cells.

neoplasm

A new and abnormal growth of tissue. Neoplasms can become BENIGN or MALIGNANT TUMORS.

nodule
A small cluster of cells. Can be benign or malignant.

Northern blot
Technique for analyzing mRNA using a DNA probe.

nuclear magnetic resonance imaging
Same as MAGNETIC RESONANCE IMAGING.

nucleic acids
Molecules composed of single- or double-strand chains of nucleotide units (bases). There are two types: DNA and RNA.

nucleus
The region of the cell that contains the chromosomes. The nuclear membrane separates the nucleus from the other region of the cell, the CYTO-PLASM.

nulliparity
Never having given birth to a child.

---

occult

O

Hidden, concealed, or undetectable; e.g., "The presence of occult tumor cannot be ruled out."

off-label drug use
Use of an FDA-approved drug by a physician to treat a disease other than that for which the drug was approved.

oligonucleotide
DNA or RNA that is two to a few hundred bases in length.

oncogene
A normal gene that when mutated can lead to uncontrolled cell division and plays a significant role in causing cancer.

oncology
The branch of medicine dealing with tumors.

p

In genetics, refers to the region of a chromosome known as the short arm. See also "q." In molecular biology, p stands for protein; e.g., "The p53 gene suppresses cell division." (The number 53 refers to the size of the protein in chemical units known as kilodaltons.) In statistics, p refers to a measure of STATISTICAL SIGNIFICANCE.

P450

See CYTOCHROME P450 ENZYMES.

palliative treatment

A treatment that relieves symptoms without curing the disease. The goal is to improve the quality of life.

palpation

The use of touch to detect evidence of disease or injury.

Pap test

A test for early detection of cancer. In cervical cancer, it involves collecting cells shed from the cervix for microscopic examination. Named after its developer, George Papanicolaou.

particle beam radiation therapy

Treatment of cancer using particulate radiation. Particulate radiation includes beams of electrons, protons, or neutrons.

PCR

See POLYMERASE CHAIN REACTION.

pelvic exam

A manual examination of female reproductive organs through the vagina and rectum.

peptide

A class of compounds consisting of a short chain of amino acids. Peptides have two or more amino acids but are smaller and simpler than proteins. In the body, peptides serve as hormones and to transmit nerve impulses. Others regulate cells in the immune, endocrine, and digestive systems. Fragments of proteins are also referred to as peptides.

peptide bond

The chemical bond that links amino acids in peptides and proteins.

photodynamic therapy (PDT)

Treatment of disease using drugs that are activated by light, usually ultraviolet or laser light.

placebo
An inactive substance or dummy pill given to participants in some studies testing the efficacy of a new drug. Also, an inert or innocuous substance given to a patient to satisfy the patient's mental need for medication.

polycyclic aromatic hydrocarbon (PAH)
A broad class of organic chemicals in petroleum and coal tar, many of which are potent carcinogens. PAH molecules all have one or more hexagonal rings composed of carbon and hydrogen atoms. Examples include benzene, benzopyrene, and dimethylbenzanthracene.

polymerase chain reaction (PCR)
A laboratory technique that allows specific DNA sequences to be duplicated a million or more times in a few hours. RT-PCR (reverse transcriptase-PCR) allows researchers to make millions of DNA copies of a messenger RNA for study. The enzyme reverse transcriptase is used first to make a copy of the mRNA in the form of DNA. The PCR reaction is then used to make millions of copies of the DNA for study.

polyp
A tumor with a stem or pedicle. Usually benign, but sometimes cancerous.

polypeptide
A chain of amino acids joined by peptide bonds.

ppm/ppb (parts per million/parts per billion)
Used to describe the concentration of one substance with respect to another. For example, a chemical might be said to be present in water at a level of 35 parts per million parts (of water). The "parts" of each are described in similar units of weight or volume. In this case, there would be 35 grams of chemical per million grams of water. 1 ppm is the same as 1 milligram per liter of water (1 ml of pure water weighs one gram).

precancerous
A growth that is likely to become cancerous.

preclinical testing/research
Phase of drug development in which a potential drug is tested on animals. Substances that look sufficiently promising in preclinical testing often go on for testing in humans through clinical trials.

prevalence
The total number of cases of a disease in a given population during a specific period of time. See INCIDENCE.

prevention

Can be primary, secondary, or tertiary. Primary prevention refers to minimizing exposure to things that cause cancer. Secondary prevention refers to early detection of cancer. Tertiary prevention refers to the treatment of cancer.

primary tumor

The original tumor in a cancer patient.

prognosis

Predicted course and outcome of a disease, and the likelihood of recovery.

prokaryotic

Refers to organisms that have a single circular chromosome that is not surrounded by a nuclear membrane. Prokaryotic organisms also lack membrane-bound organelles such as mitochondria, chloroplasts, and lysosomes. Examples are bacteria and blue-green algae. Compare with EUKARYOTIC.

promoter

In cancer: a chemical or substance that is not itself carcinogenic but that assists in the development of the disease. Promoters play an important role in chemical carcinogenesis. They are thought to stimulate cell division and reduce the effectiveness of DNA repair in initiated cells (cells in which the DNA has been damaged by a chemical carcinogen). In molecular biology: a region of DNA that initiates TRANSCRIPTION of a gene.

prospective study

Epidemiological study that follows a group of people forward in time to observe an outcome. Prospective studies are used to follow the people exposed to risk factor, or patients with a disease or who have received a particular treatment. Compare with RETROSPECTIVE STUDY.

prostate

A solid, oblong gland that lies at the base of the bladder in males. About the size of a walnut, it surrounds the urethra and neck of the bladder and has ducts that open into the urethra. It secretes a milky fluid that maintains semen at pH 7.

prosthesis

An artificial organ or part. Examples include artificial eyes, hands, or extremities.

protein

A molecule made up of one or more chains of amino acids (i.e., POLYPEP-TIDES). Most proteins have 50 to several thousand amino acids. Molecules consisting of only a few amino acids are called peptides.

protein engineering

Changing one or more specific amino acids in a protein by altering the gene for that protein. It is used to make a protein more or less stable and to change its specificity for an enzyme.

protein kinase

An enzyme that adds phosphate groups to itself or to other proteins. Adding a phosphate group can make a protein more or less active.

protein synthesis

The production of a protein by a cell. It occurs in two stages known as TRANSCRIPTION and TRANSLATION.

protocol/research protocol

Guidelines and rule book used by physicians participating in a clinical trial. The protocol outlines how the study is to be done, the kinds of pa-tients that can be accepted, how the treatment is to be administered, and how a patient's outcome is to be recorded.

proto-oncogene

The name for any healthy gene that when mutated may lead to cancer. The mutated version of the gene is referred to as an oncogene. Proto-oncogenes are genes that normally control such things as cell growth, cell division, and the production of growth factors.

p value

See STATISTICAL SIGNIFICANCE.

---

q

Refers to the region of a chromosome known as the long arm. See also "p."

quality of life

Evaluation of the effects of an illness or treatment on a patient's ability to enjoy life.

rad
A measurement of radiation absorbed by tissues. Acronym for "radiation absorbed dose."

radiation
A general term for the propagation of energy through space. Includes emissions from luminous bodies, fluorescing substances, X-ray tubes, and radioactive elements.

radiation sensitizer
A chemical that is taken up by cancer cells that makes them more susceptible to the cell-killing effects of radiation therapy.

radiation therapy
Use of penetrating rays or subatomic particles to treat disease, particularly cancer. Types of radiation include X-rays and gamma rays, alpha and beta particles, and electron beams. Commonly used radioactive elements include cobalt, iodine, radium, iridium, and cesium.

radioactive implant
A tiny "seed" of radioactive material surgically placed in or near a tumor. The implant is a source of radiation to destroy cancer cells. Used in BRACHYTHERAPY.

radioisotope
A radioactive form of an element.

radionuclide
A radioactive atom that gives off gamma rays as it disintegrates.

radiotherapy
Same as RADIATION THERAPY.

radical treatment
Aggressive treatment.

receptor proteins
In molecular biology, molecular switches that trigger some change to occur within cells. Receptors are activated to bring about their change by a second molecule, known as a LIGAND, that binds to them. Receptors are highly specific for certain ligands. Ligands include drugs, hormones, neurotransmitters, and growth factors. See CELL-SURFACE RECEPTORS.

receptors, steroid
These are receptors that are located within cells. They are activated by steroid HORMONES (sex hormones and certain hormones produced by the adrenal gland).

recombinant DNA technology
Collectively, the laboratory techniques that allow researchers to cut genes from a chromosome in one organism (such as a human) and splice them into the chromosome of another organism (such as a bacterium). Also allow researchers to isolate and modify genes, and make strands of DNA based on patterns provided by bits or molecules of RNA (see cDNA) for locating genes on chromosomes.

rectum
Last segment of the large intestine, about 5 inches long. Extends from the end of the colon to the anus.

recurrence
Return of disease after a period free of the disease's signs or symptoms.

regimen
A course or program of treatment.

regional involvement
Cancer that has spread from the organ in which it originated to neighboring organs or lymph nodes.

regulatory protein
A protein that binds to DNA and, alone or in conjunction with other proteins, turns off or turns on a gene. Same as a DNA-binding protein.

relapse
Same as RECURRENCE.

remission
Lessening of intensity or disappearance of symptoms or disease.

retinoids
The natural and synthetic analogs of vitamin A. Retinoids are being investigated as chemotherapy for and chemoprevention of cancer.

retrospective study
An epidemiological study that looks backward in time. Retrospective studies use medical records and interviews with patients who already have a disease to search for a common cause or risk factor. Compare with PROSPECTIVE STUDY.

retroviruses

Common name for viruses that carry their genetic information in the form of RNA rather than DNA. Once inside the cell, the retroviruses use the enzyme reverse transcriptase to make a DNA copy of their RNA genes (hence the name "retro" virus; the usual process is to make RNA from a DNA template). The DNA copy then becomes part of a host chromosome. Many retroviruses induce a variety of cancers in lower animals. In humans, retroviruses are responsible for causing AIDS and have been linked to certain leukemias and lymphomas. The discovery of the enzyme reverse transcriptase was major factor in the development of RE-COMBINANT DNA TECHNOLOGY.

reverse transcriptase

Enzyme used by retroviruses to make DNA from RNA. See RETRO-VIRUSES.

ribosomes

Extremely small structures in the cell made from a type of RNA (ribosomal RNA or rRNA). They attach to messenger RNA and read the genetic code during protein synthesis. See TRANSLATION. Ribosomes can be found individually or in clusters called polyribosomes or polysomes.

risk

The risk of developing a disease is usually described in terms of relative risk. Relative risk is calculated by dividing the frequency of mortality in a group exposed to a carcinogen or risk factor by the frequency of mortality in an unexposed group.

risk factors

Elements in the lifestyle, environment, and genetic makeup of an individual that are thought to increase the chance of developing disease. Cancer risk factors include smoking, alcohol use, a diet high in fat, and exposure to ultraviolet light.

risk reduction

Reducing the number or the magnitude of risk factors for a disease, thereby reducing the odds that one will develop the disease.

roentgen ray

Same as X-RAY.

RNA

Ribonucleic acid. One of two groups of nucleic acids, the other being DNA. There are three forms of RNA in the cell: MESSENGER RNA or mRNA, ribosomal RNA or rRNA (see RIBOSOMES), and TRANSFER RNA or tRNA.

RT-PCR
Reverse transcriptase polymerase chain reaction. See POLYMERASE CHAIN REACTION.

---

sarcoma
Cancer that arises from connective tissue including bone, cartilage, and muscle. Sarcomas can also occur the liver, lungs, spleen, kidneys, and bladder.

scintigraphy
A diagnostic imaging technique that uses a gamma camera and radionuclides to make scans of many organ systems including heart, bone, brain, thyroid, and kidneys. The resulting image is called a scintigram.

screening
Testing of large groups of people to identify the presence of a particular disease or of risk factors associated with the disease. Screenings are done for cancers of the cervix, breast, prostate, and colon.

secondary tumor
A tumor that develops from cells shed by the primary tumor; a metastatic tumor.

second-degree relatives
Those that share a quarter of your genes (grandparents, aunts, uncles).

sensitivity
The probability that a test will identify patients who have a disease or condition. A test with high sensitivity produces a low number of falsely negative results. Compare with SPECIFICITY.

side effects
Effects or actions of a drug other than those desired. Usually said of adverse effects or toxicities of a drug such as nausea, dizziness, or headaches.

sigmoidoscopy
Examination of the the sigmoid colon with a sigmoidoscope. The sigmoid colon is the S-shaped region of the large intestine that lies within the pelvis and extends between the descending colon and the rectum.

signs (of disease)
Visible or measurable indications of disease such as fever. Objective indicators of disease. See SYMPTOMS.

somatic cells
The nonreproductive cells that make up the body. Mutations in genes of somatic cells are not passed on to a person's children. See GERM CELLS.

Southern blot
Technique using a DNA probe to analyze the structure of a gene.

specificity
The probability that a test will be negative in people who do NOT have a disease or condition. A test with high specificity produces a low number of falsely positive results. Compare with SENSITIVITY.

squamous cell carcinoma
A common form of skin cancer that metastasizes readily but is highly curable if caught early. When it occurs at other sites such as the lung and stomach, it is often untreatable and deadly.

staging
Process of classifying tumors with respect to malignancy and potential for responding to treatment.

statistical significance
A measure of the probability that a difference seen during an experiment occurred by chance. This probability is referred to as the p value. A p value of 0.05 ($p = .05$) indicates a 1-in-20 probability that the result occurred by chance; when $p = 0.01$, there is an estimated 1-in-100 probability that the result occurred by chance. A value of $p = 0.05$ or less is arbitrarily and customarily used as a measure of statistical significance.

stem cell
A cell that gives rise to other cells. Hematopoietic stem cells found in the bone marrow, for example, give rise to red and white blood cells.

stoma
A small opening; an artificial opening between two body cavities or between a body cavity or passage and the surface of the body.

stool blood test
Simple test for the presence of hidden blood in feces. Important in the early detection of colon and rectal cancer.

surrogate marker
A measure of the outcome of a treatment other than mortality or survival. Examples of surrogate markers for cancer include reduction in tumor size or a change in level of a tumor marker.

survival rate

Observed (or absolute) survival rate: the actual proportion of people alive after some specified time period. **Relative survival rate**: The proportion of people estimated to survive after other causes of death are taken into account. Relative survival rates are therefore higher than observed survival rates.

symptoms

Indicators of disease that are reported by the patient and cannot usually be observed or measured (such as pain). Subjective indicators of disease. See SIGNS. Some, however, consider symptoms to be any indicator of disease, whether subjective or objective.

synthesis

Making complex substances from simpler ones; making proteins from amino acids, for example.

synthesize

To produce something by synthesis.

systemic

Pertaining to the entire body rather than just to a part.

T cells (T lymphocytes)

T

Lymphocytes that mature in the thymus gland. T cells recognize antigens on cell surfaces. They form the branch of the immune system responsible for the CELL-MEDIATED IMMUNE RESPONSE.

telomere/telomerase

A telomere is a length of DNA at each tip of a chromosome that is essential for DNA replication. Teleomeres also seem to serve as a kind of biological clock that determines how many times a cell will divide. Each time a chromosome replicates prior to cell division, a bit of each telomere is lopped off. When the telomeres are shortened to a critical length, the cell stops dividing and becomes senescent or dies by APOPTOSIS. During development, when continued cell division is needed for the growing fetus, the shortening of telomeres is prevented by the enzyme telomerase, which rebuilds the shortened ends. The gene that produces telomerase is then turned off in most cells at birth. Evidence is emerging, however, that the telomerase gene is reactivated in many types of cancer, and that the enzyme may be important for continued division of tumor cells. This suggests that loss of control of the telomerase gene may contribute to the development of some cancers.

three-dimensional treatment planning

A means of precisely locating a tumor that requires intricate radiation treatment. Uses a computer to compile a three-dimensional image of the tumor from a series of CT scans (see COMPUTED TOMOGRAPHY SCAN).

tissue

A group of similar cells, their products, and intercellular material, specialized to perform a specific function. The major types of tissues are epithelial, muscular, skeletal, connective, glandular, and nervous.

toxoid

A toxin that has been rendered harmless. Diphtheria toxoid, or some other toxoid, is sometimes used as a component in cancer vaccines to help cause an immune reaction to the vaccine.

trans- and trans-acting

Prefix meaning across or beyond. In molecular biology: a REGULATORY PROTEIN that can act at a great distance, even on another chromosome.

transcription

The first stage of protein synthesis during which the cell makes an RNA copy of a gene. This RNA—MESSENGER RNA (mRNA)—carries the imprint of the gene from the NUCLEUS to the CYTOPLASM. There, RIBOSOMES combine with it for the second stage of protein synthesis, TRANSLATION.

transcription activator

A protein molecule that initiates TRANSCRIPTION of a gene. It thereby activates the gene. Some of the proteins produced by oncogenes are transcription activators.

transduction

Using a virus to introduce a gene into a cell.

transfection

Using mechanical means to introduce a gene into a cell or organism. Such cells or organisms are said to be transfected.

transfer RNA (tRNA)

A type of ribonucleic acid (RNA) that brings amino acids to the RIBOSOME during protein synthesis.

transformation

A change in the form or function of a cell when its genes are modified. A cell is transformed when a cell becomes cancerous or when a gene is added through genetic engineering to give the cell a different property.

translation

In cell biology, translation is the second of two stages of protein sythesis. It occurs when MESSENGER RNA (mRNA), which carries an imprint of a gene, combines with RIBOSOMES in the CYTOPLASM. Each ribosome moves along the mRNA molecule "reading" the GENETIC CODE. The code reveals the order of amino acids that make up the protein. The amino acids are brought to the ribosome as needed by TRANSFER RNA or tRNA. The ribosome continues moving along the mRNA, and one amino acid is added to the previous one in a lengthening chain that in the end forms the complete protein.

translational research

Laboratory research that is done to solve a problem or answer a question relating to the cause, prevention, or treatment of disease. The name in medicine for the interaction of BASIC RESEARCH and CLINICAL RESEARCH.

tumor

Literally, a swelling. A new and spontaneous growth of tissue that forms an abnormal mass. Usually used in reference to solid tumors, but in a more general sense the term can also include non-solid tumors such as leukemia. Solid tumors can be BENIGN or MALIGNANT.

tumorigenic

Used to describe something that causes tumors, especially malignant tumors.

tumor infiltrating lymphocytes (TILs)

Lymphocytes that have invaded a tumor.

tumor markers

Tumor-associated markers are substances in a patient's blood serum that when present in elevated levels suggest the presence of a malignancy. Examples include carcinoembryonic antigen (CEA) for colon, lung, breast, and ovarian cancer; alpha-fetoprotein for testicular cancer; and prostate specific antigen (PSA) for prostate cancer. They are usually proteins found on the surface of cancer cells and shed into the bloodstream. Tumor-susceptibility markers are genes such as mutated tumor suppressor genes that may indicate a person is particularly susceptible to particular cancers (i.e., they are at higher than normal risk for the disease).

tumor necrosis factor (TNF)

A major cytokine produced by certain white blood cells (macrophages). It kills certain neoplastic cells, has antiviral activity, and has hormone-like influences on white blood cells and cells lining blood vessels.

tumor virus
A virus that produces malignant tumors.

---

ultrasound
Sound waves that are inaudible to the human ear. Their frequency ranges from 20,000 to 10 billion (10^9) cycles per second. Ultrasound travels through different tissues at different velocities, enabling its use for making diagnostic images of body organs. Ultrasound is also used to produce heat for the treatment of certain cancers.

up-regulation
Increase in the activity of a gene.

---

vaccine/cancer vaccine
A solution containing killed or weakened viruses or bacteria, or parts of them, given to stimulate immunity to a specific infectious disease. A cancer vaccine is an experimental treatment that uses killed cancer cells or a protein unique to cancer cells to stimulate immunity to a tumor. Often, the protein alone is not enough to provoke an immune response, so it is linked to a second protein—an adjuvant—that will provoke a strong immune response.

vein
Vessel that carries blood to the heart. Compare with ARTERY.

viruses
Parasitic organisms that consist of little more than a strand of either DNA or RNA (but not both) surrounded by a protein coat or capsid. The number of genes they contain can range from five to several hundred. RNA viruses are also known as RETROVIRUSES. Viruses are not visible by ordinary light microscopy and must be viewed by electron microscopy.

Western blot
Technique for identifying a specific protein using an antibody coupled to a radioactive isotope, an enzyme, or a fluorescent dye.

wild type
The usual or typical form of an organism in nature as compared to a mutated form. The term is also applied to a gene and its protein; e.g., "Wild-type WP1 protein can inhibit the growth of cultured cells derived from a human Wilms' tumor."

X-ray
High-energy radiation useful at low levels to diagnose disease and at high levels to treat cancer. Also called roentgen rays. X-rays are usually produced electrically, that is, without use of a radioactive source.

zinc fingers
Finger-like projections on some REGULATORY PROTEINS that enable the protein to attach to DNA. The fingers insert between twists in the DNA helix. The orientation and makeup of the fingers allow the protein to attach to a precise location on the DNA molecule (i.e., to a precise location on a particular gene). The attachment of a regulatory protein like these turns genes on or off, depending on the gene. The name zinc finger comes from the fact that these projections in the protein molecule form around an atom of zinc.

Suggested Reading

American Cancer Society Textbook of Clinical Oncology. 1995. The American Cancer Society.

Cancer Facts and Figures. American Cancer Society. Updated annually, this booklet is available free from local American Cancer Society offices.

Cancer: Principles and Practice of Oncology. V.S. DeVita, Jr., S. Hellman, and S.A. Rosenberg. 1993. Philadelphia: J.B. Lippincott. One of the leading textbooks on cancer diagnosis and treatment.

Frontiers. Magazine published by The Ohio State University cancer program. Contains substantive articles on cancer research and issues of national interest.

Genes and the Biology of Cancer. Harold Varmus and Robert A. Weinberg. 1993. New York: Scientific American Library.

The Hospice Handbook: A Complete Guide. Larry Beresford. 1993. Little, Brown. A good overview of hospice care and hospice programs. 165 pages.

Introduction to Molecular Medicine. Dennis W. Rose. 1992. New York: Springer-Verlag. This small book (174 pages) provides concise descriptions of the concepts of molecular biology and the techniques of recombinant DNA technology, and how they are applied to the areas of infectious disease, genetic disease, cancer, and environmental medicine.

The Machinery of Life. David S. Goodsell. 1992. New York: Springer-Verlag. A small book (140 pages) for non-scientists about the biochemistry of the cell.

Merck Manual of Diagnosis and Therapy. Published by Merck Sharp and Dohme Research Laboratories.

Natural Obsessions: The Search for the Oncogene. Natalie Angier. 1988. Warner Books. Story by a leading science reporter of the race to isolate and clone oncogenes. Provides insights into how basic research is done.

Taber's Cyclopedic Medical Dictionary. Philadelphia: F.A. Davis Company.

The Transformed Cell: Unlocking the Mysteries of Cancer. Steven A. Rosenberg and John M. Barry. 1992. New York: G.P. Putnam's Sons. Rosenberg is NCI's chief of surgery and the founder of immunotherapy for cancer. This autobiographical work provides insights into how medical advances move from the laboratory to the patient's bedside.

Index

and single-gene mutations 45
and socioeconomic status 36
susceptibility 38, 45
and tobacco 9, 72
treatment of 73–74. *See also* Chemotherapy; Immunotherapy
vaccines against 54
Cancer Information Service 4, 65
Cancer Study Groups. *See* Clinical Trials
Cooperative Groups
Cancer study groups 22, 24
CancerFax 4
CancerNet 4
Cansearch 5
Carbon tetrachloride 64
Carcinogen testing 49
Carcinogenesis 6–7
Carcinogens
asbestos 7, 29
chemical 6–7, 64
chlorine 11, 64
dust 7, 9
electron, proton, neutron beams 7
environmental pollution 29, 64
epigenetic 95
food 9
gamma rays 7
genotoxic 97
heavy metals 29
human (table) 10
identification of 8, 49–53
introduced during food preparation 29
naturally occurring 29
tobacco smoke 9
ultraviolet light 7, 80–81
viral 7
X-rays 7
Carcinomas 1
hepatocellular 82
in situ 76
nasopharyngeal 28, 82
Carotenoids 29
Case control studies 8, 71
Causes of cancer. *See* Cancer: causes of
CD (Cluster of differentiation) 90
CEA (carcinoembryonic antigen) 75
Cell 13–18
cycle 17
cytoplasm 13
differentiation and dedifferentiation 17
division 39, 57
membrane 13, 14–15, 57
lipid bilayer 14
nucleus 13
Cell-mediated immune response 91
Cervical cancer 35, 84
Chemotherapy 19–21, 74
adjuvant 19
and the cell cycle 19
experimental 20–21
and healthy cells 19

Chlorambucil 11
Chlordane 29
Chlorofluorocarbons (CFCs) 64, 80–81
Cholesterol 14, 29
Chromosome(s) 13, 42
and DNA (figure) 42
defects 42, 57
in eggs and sperm 42
Chronic bioassay 51, 52
Cis- 92
Cisplatin 20
Clinical trials 22–23
Clinical trials cooperative groups 22, 24
c-myc gene 40, 42
Codeine 62
Codon 66
Cohort studies 8, 71
Colchicine 20
Colon cancer 28, 44, 56, 64, 79
Colorectal cancer 44
Community Clinical Oncology Program
(CCOP) 24
Complementary base pairing 31–32, 66
Comprehensive Cancer Centers, NCI-
designated 93
Computed tomography (CT) 26, 74
Conformational therapy 74
Consumer Products Safety
Commission 49
Contraceptives 11, 47
CT (computed tomography) scan 26, 74
"Curing" cancer 25
Cyclic adenosine monophosphate
(cAMP) 58
Cyclin 39
Cyclophosphamide 11, 19
Cyclosporine 11
Cytokines 54
Cytoplasm 13
Cytosine 31

D

DDT 29
Diagnosis 26–27, 36
Diet 9, 28–30
Diethylstilbestrol 11
Digital rectal exam 65
Dioxin 64
DNA 13, 31–32, 40
and cancer 6–7, 7
and chromosomes 42
and complementary base pairing 31–32
and protein synthesis 66
and radiation therapy 73
replication (figure) 32
structure (figure) 32
DNA binding proteins 58
DNA helicase 32
DNA ligase 32
DNA polymerase 32
DNA primase 32

Vinblastine   20
Vincristine   20
Vinyl chloride   52
Viruses, as cause of cancer   7, 11, 82–84
Vitamins   28
   A   21, 30
   C   29
   E   29

W
Warts, anal-genital   82–84
World Health Organization   49, 62, 70

X
X-rays   7, 11, 26, 73

Z
Zeolite   9
Zinc finger   121